COMBAT PROFILE:
MUSTANG

The P-51 Merlin Mustang
in World War 2

COMBAT PROFILE:
MUSTANG

The P-51 Merlin Mustang
in World War 2

ROGER A. FREEMAN

LONDON
IAN ALLAN LTD

Acknowledgements

This book has been made possible through material and information contributed by several generous individuals. They are: Edward Bahlhorn, William Fleming, Steve Gotts, A. Hiltgen, Patricia Keen, Philip Knowles, Ian Mactaggart, David Mayor, Danny Morris, Eric Munday, Merle Olmsted, Robert Riemensnider, Ben Simpronio, Curtis Smart, Stan Staples, Hugh Sutton, and George Vanden Heuval.

I wish to record my sincere thanks to all, and also to Jean Freeman and Bruce Robertson for editorial assistance, and Norman Ottaway for his excellent drawings.

Roger A. Freeman   *Dedham 1989*

Sole distributors for the USA

Motorbooks International
Publishers & Wholesalers Inc
Osceola, Wisconsin 54020, USA ®

First published 1989

ISBN 0 7110 1807 3

Published by Ian Allan Ltd, Shepperton, Surrey; and printed by Ian Allan Printing Ltd at their works at Coombelands in Runnymede, England

Contents

Below:
For night operations some RAF Mustangs had a bracket attached to the fuselag to shield the pilot's eyes from the engine exhaust flames. WO Newton of No 154 Squadron (top right) uses the bracket as a perch. P. Knowles

Introduction

The North American P-51 Mustang is one of the most successful piston-engined fighter aircraft and, over the years, has received acclaim in many publications. This compilation is neither a development study nor an operational history of the type, aspects already given comprehensive coverage in several books. Here, the object is to give an appreciation of what was required of a pilot flying the Merlin-powered Mustang in combat operations, with an understanding of the aircraft's vices and virtues. This is based on the extensive records deposited in United States and British archives and the opinions of men who flew the Mustang in various theatres of war.

Named Mustang by the British and designated P-51 by the United States Army Air Forces, the North American NA-73 fighter was one of the most successful aircraft of World War 2. This attribution is based upon its use in establishing and maintaining air supremacy over enemy territory in Europe during the final critical phases of that conflict. The developed aircraft gave excellent performance with exceptional endurance and led to the Mustang's role as the premier Allied fighter for long range escort and strike operations.

The design and prototype were produced in a remarkably short time — some six months — by obtaining advanced data from the Curtiss-Wright company and the National Advisory Committee for Aeronautics. This was to meet British stipulations on urgency. The prototype first flew on 20 November 1940 and production aircraft were arriving in the United Kingdom a year later. Initially there was little USAAF interest in the Mustang as it had been designed and financed for the British, but once the type's escort fighter potential was appreciated the Mustang received priority production.

As supplied to the Royal Air Force, the original Mustang had an Allison liquid-cooled engine with a low-altitude rating. Above 15,000ft power output decreased as height was increased, slowing the rate of climb. For this reason the RAF considered the aircraft outclassed by the main enemy interceptors, and used the Mustang to equip its fighter-reconnaissance squadrons with a low altitude mission. A force of 16 such squadrons was established by 1943 with some 250 Mustangs.

The advanced aerodynamics of the Mustang design impressed the British, who suggested the installation of the powerful, high-altitude-rated Rolls-Royce Merlin engine. Successful conversions were carried out both in the UK and USA, with production arrangements made for the P-51B, the model designation for the Mustang fitted with the Packard-built version of the Merlin.

In the autumn of 1943, the first Merlin-engined Mustangs began reaching the UK and the operational debut of this model was on 1 December that year. Subsequently, most of the USAAF long range fighter units were equipped with Merlin Mustangs — the P-51B, C, D and K models — and the type was also employed by the RAF as the Mustang III and IV.

The Allison-engined version continued to serve in the fighter-reconnaissance role with the RAF (as the Mustang I and II) until replacements were exhausted. Of the original Allison Mustang squadrons, only one survived to the end of hostilities in Europe. The small number of Allison-powered Mustangs acquired by the USAAF as P-51 and P-51A also served chiefly in the fighter-reconnaissance role, although those sent to the China-Burma-India Theatre of Operations were often used for long range escort. Another version of the Allison-engined Mustang was the A-36A, little more than a P-51A fitted with bomb shackles and dive brakes under each wing for employment as a dive-bomber. Again the production run was small and most of the 500 produced went to six squadrons in the Mediterranean Theatre of Operations.

Total Allison-engined Mustang production for the RAF was 762, while the USAAF received 818, of which 499 were A-36As. Merlin Mustang production ran to 13,440 P-51B, C, D and K models and their variants. Most other model designations did not get beyond the prototype stage. One that did was the P-51H, a complete redesign intended to reduce airframe weight and improve rate of climb. The 555 P-51Hs did not see action in World War 2 but equipped several USAAF and reserve units during the immediate postwar years. A unique long range development entering limited postwar production was the P-82 Twin-Mustang. Basically, this was two Mustangs joined together to make a twin-engined, two-pilot fighter for extreme long range flight.

Mustangs served with several national air forces during the post-World War 2 period and were also used extensively in the Korean conflict of 1950-53 in a ground support role. The P-51D was the model employed by USAF, South Korean and South African Air Force units, while the Royal Australian Air Force used the Australian-built version of this model.

More Mustangs have endured than any other single World War 2 combat aircraft. Near a half-century after the design was originally conceived some 200 are still being flown — but in peaceful airshow or racing roles.

1
Combat Sortie – Escort

What was involved in flying a Mustang on a combat sortie? The following account describes in detail the actions and experiences of an American pilot on a long-range bomber escort mission over Germany. The piloting and operational procedures are typical of all such sorties but the individual experiences related are, of course, reactions to particular circumstances.

A blinding light and a tug on the shoulder brings 1Lt George Vanden Heuvel abruptly out of sleep's oblivion. 'Wake up, Van: breakfast at oh-eight-thirty; briefing at oh-nine hundred.' The Duty Officer removes his torch from the pilot's face and moves further up the hut to repeat the performance at another bed. As Lt Vanden Heuvel collects his senses, three other men are awakened before the Duty Officer departs, switching on the light as he closes the inner door behind him. Those he has summoned gradually stagger out of bed and commence dressing. Other men in the hut, who have been awakened by the lights and movements, sleepily wisecrack before turning over: 'Get one for me today, Van.' 'If you see Hitler, tell him I've quit.'

Lt Vanden Heuvel pulls on standard GI trousers and shirt over his wool underclothing. He tops this with a fur-collared B-15 flying jacket. Wool socks and GI shoes are worn: the GI shoe is a leather, lace-up, ankle-covering boot. As he straps on his wristwatch he notes the time is just past 08.00 on this late November morning in 1944. There is a chill in the hut, the tortoise stove having burned itself out several hours ago. Topcoats go on as the four pilots make for the communal ablutions building that stands in the centre of the cluster of Nissen huts that represent 'home' for the men of the 376th Fighter Squadron. It is still only half-light, but the sky is clear and the night's frost has been hard enough to put a crust on the usual mud beside the concrete pathways. As eyes become accustomed to the gloom, the silhouettes of other 'tin' huts are visible, as are the dark shapes of oaks in a neighbouring hedgerow. Like all the living sites at this station, that of the 376th Fighter Squadron is dispersed amongst meadows in the English countryside. The United States Army

Air Forces Station 165, Little Walden, like most of the operational airfields in the United Kingdom, has been built to a wartime plan on what, until 1942, was farmland.

Washed and shaved, the four pilots make their way on foot from the squadron location along another path to the communal site where the mess hall is situated. Blackout rules, so the only lights come from torches stabbing through the darkness in the entrances of buildings. Men from other huts are also bound for breakfast. Cigarettes glow; talk is muted.

Inside the mess hall all is light and noise. Two fresh eggs, done as requested, hash browns (fried potato), toast and coffee soon fortify constitutions. Casual conversation swells; no one speculates about the operation ahead although the volume of engine noise high above indicates a bomber escort.

By 08.50hrs most appetites are satisfied and 50 pilots climb on to the back of four 'Six by Six' trucks waiting outside the mess hall. The pilots are young. At 27, George Vanden Heuvel is five years older than the average, having been an instructor pilot in the United States before assignment to this station as a replacement. This is one of those rare mornings in an English winter when the sun is not hidden by cloud. No doubt, it aids the notably brighter mood of the pilots; no tricky flying through overcast today.

After a half-mile along winding roads the trucks reach the large assembly of buildings beside the airfield and stop outside a Quanset complex consisting of two of these large curved roof structures placed as wings to a third. The occupants of the trucks tumble out and make for the open double doors, passing through the open blackout curtains into a hallway. Everyone crowds around a small table where two clerks check off each man's name, allowing him to proceed through the adjacent door into the briefing room. An MP stands guard at this door to see no unauthorised personnel gain admittance.

The briefing room is one wing of the complex. Rows of canvas-backed tubular framed chairs are situated on either side of a central aisle. At the far end from the entrance is a podium with the wall behind covered by a large map of North-West Europe; for the moment most of this map is hidden from view behind a drape. At one side of the podium a large blackboard is positioned and this carries chalk figures on engine start times and other crucial data.

Below:
This well-folded 18×30in, four-colour, High Altitude Fighter Map was used for the mission. The route was not marked in case the map fell into enemy hands.

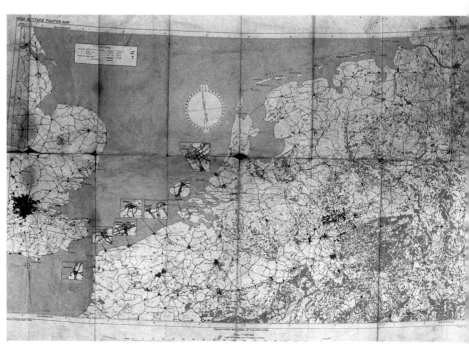

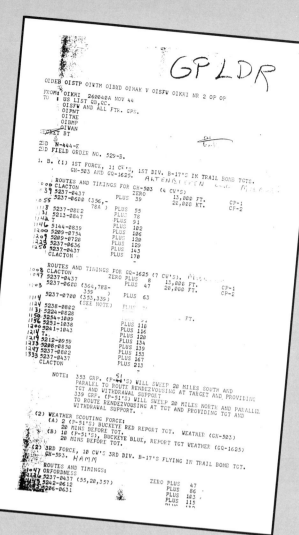

Above and right:
Order for the mission is received by the 361st Group by teletype.
Via I. Mactaggart

Below:
**The Briefing Officer: 'Any Questions?'
There were usually a few.**

The hubbub of voices grows as the pilots take their seats and the room fills. The row ceases immediately an officer at the podium calls the men to attention. Down the aisle marches the Group Commander and the mission leader for the day, followed by the Weather Officer. The CO mounts the stage and calls: 'At ease gentlemen'. Meanwhile, the Group Operations Officer has pulled back the curtain from the wall map to reveal coloured ribbons stretching from England out across the North Sea and Holland into north central Germany. These indicate the routes of the bomber and fighter formations for the coming operation. The Group Operations Officer starts the briefing by giving an outline of the day's objectives. The heavy bombers are being sent to attack oil and transportation targets. The three squadrons of the 361st Fighter Group — of which Van's is one — are to provide escort for the leading wing of B-24 Liberators which are to bomb the synthetic oil installations at Misburg, not far from Hanover. As this is believed to be the only large refinery in the area still active, there is a reasonable chance that Luftwaffe fighters may rise to challenge the mission. Van notes that the particular Liberators they have to escort can be identified by black tails with vertical and horizonal white bars. The 361st is scheduled to rendezvous with the bombers at 11.19hrs over The Netherlands.

Details of times and checkpoints are given and the areas of possible enemy interception suggested. The Group Operations Officer takes less than 10 minutes to make his points and hands over to the Weather Officer. With the aid of a large diagram which he pins to the blackboard, the Weather Officer delivers his prognosis and known conditions present in the area of operations. Finally, the air leader for the mission gives instructions about flight procedures based on the requirements of the mission, finishing with a time check. This involves every pilot synchronising his wristwatch — a special standard issue — on the leader's. With watch hands adjusted, the leader calls 'Hack' for the start button to be pressed. Briefing concludes with a few words of encouragement and a joke from the air leader.

As the pilots leave the briefing room a sergeant, standing in the doorway, gives each one a Mission Data Card on which are carried the radio callsigns and other signals information for the day, crucial times and checkpoints. Some of this is given in coded form as the cards will be carried for reference on the flight and there is always the possibility that this information may fall into enemy hands early in the mission.

The pilots now make for their Squadron Ready-Rooms in other

Above:
Leaving for the planes: these fighter pilots have already donned their parachute packs. M. Olmsted

wings of the same building complex. Part of each Ready-Room is a personal equipment store with lockers. George Vanden Heuvel takes off his B-15 jacket and drapes it over a chair before he retrieves various items of flying attire from his locker. First he slips on and straps up the so-called Berger G-suit over the GI trousers he is wearing. Consisting of inflatable rubber cells in canvas sleeves, the G-suit fits around each leg, the thighs and the lower abdomen. A hose attachment will be connected to a vacuum outlet in the aircraft for inflating the suit automatically to impede the flow of blood when the body is subjected to severe gravitational pull in flight. Next the Summer Flying Suit — a one-piece coverall garment, which is almost standard wear despite it being far from summer weather. Zipped up, Van then goes through the careful procedure of placing specific items in certain pockets; it is essential to know instinctively where they are as there is no time for searching in an emergency. In the left breast pocket an extra clip of rounds for his .45 handgun, plus a Vick inhaler to clear any respiratory problems. In the right breast pocket, cigarettes and matches. The lower left zip leg pocket holds the Escape and Evasion Kit. Among its contents are a silk map of Germany, a compass and a Russian pass — in case it is necessary to seek Soviet-held territory in an emergency. In the lower right leg pocket, a handkerchief and a chocolate bar. There is also a special pocket with a transparent window on the right thigh into which the Mission Data Card is carefully placed so that it can be seen and

referred to during the flight. Some pilots pen the details of times and checkpoints on to the back of their left hand, maintaining that this is more convenient and easier to see than peering down into the cockpit. Van finds no need for this additional aid.

He next slips on a shoulder holster harness and positions his .45 pistol in it under his left arm. The gun is carried for personal defence if brought down in enemy territory, or bringing a swift end to one's life if trapped without any hope of escape from a blazing, fire-engulfed aircraft. In some fighter groups the carrying of personal firearms is not encouraged in the belief that they give enemy personnel an excuse to shoot captured pilots out of hand with the claim they were resisting arrest. In the 361st, however, it is the general consensus of opinion among pilots that they prefer to carry pistols.

The green, fur-collared, B-15 jacket is then slipped on again and zipped up. Over the front of this a yellow 'Mae West' B-4 life vest is strapped. The 'Mae West' has a pair of small CO_2-filled cylinders for inflation, plus emergency mouth tubes for the same purpose. Van also picks up his regulation A-11 leather flying helmet, A-14 oxygen mask, B-8 Polaroid goggles, and black flying gloves, although he will not put any of them on until going out to his aircraft. As an additional aid to evasion if forced down in enemy territory, Van wears a GI web belt to which are attached a scabbard with a 6in dagger, first aid kit, water canteen and a small drawstring bag containing long woollen underwear, two bottles of malt tablets and a miniature bottle of brandy. Apart from being a useful cutting tool, the dagger knife also serves as a means of quickly deflating the seat dinghy or G-suit should these malfunction — something which was rare but not unknown.

Left:
361st Fighter Group pilots in a weapons carrier, relieved to be on their way.
U. Drew

Van's next step is to collect his parachute pack — which has the inflatable rubber dinghy attached — from the counter in the parachute room, an annexe to the same building. Some pilots prefer to leave the dinghy pack in their aircraft instead of carrying it back and forth. It also provides the crew chief with a seat cushion when he performs engine run-ups and other tests on the aircraft. Returning with his parachute to sit in the Squadron Ready-Room, Van talks to the fellow pilots, in particular to Lt Walter Kozicki, for whom he is to act as wingman. The majority of pilots smoke, and this is a last opportunity for a quick draw before the Duty Officer calls for all to go to the trucks. It is now 09.30hrs and the pilots file out carrying their parachutes. A number of 'Six by Six' trucks and Dodge Command cars are waiting on the concrete apron outside the building with their engines running. There must not be any risk of failure to start an engine; the time schedule is tight. Van and the other members of his squadron clamber up over the tailgate

into the back of a truck and sit on the low benches that run along each side. The driver's shouted question 'Where to?' brings the response: '376th'. The truck moves off into the bright morning, turns out on to the airfield perimeter track and heads for the far side. As it picks up speed the cold draughts of air coming in through the gaps in the canvas covering the truck cause the pilots to huddle forward. The 376th dispersal area lies at the extreme northwest corner of Little Walden, a loop taxiway lined with 18 loop hardstandings on which all the squadron's force of 34 P-51s are parked. Little Walden was originally built as a bomber airfield to British Class 'A' standard and, while the buildings are all utility and the accommodation spartan, the runways, perimeter track and aircraft dispersals are all of concrete construction. This is a distinct advantage in that the 361st is not troubled with mud as found on some other 'grass surface' fighter airfields.

The distance round the perimeter track to the 376th dispersals is nearly two miles and the pilots are glad to get out of the draughty trucks. Van is dropped at a P-51 which carries the markings 'E9' on one side of the fuselage star insignia and the letter 'L'

with a bar underneath on the other side. The 'E9' identifies the 376th Squadron and the 'L' is the aircraft identity within the squadron. The reason for the bar is that this is the second aircraft 'L' in the 376th, where there are more than 26 assigned aircraft and thus a fully absorbed alphabet. E9:L is George Vanden Heuvel's 'personal' aircraft which he flies whenever it is in serviceable condition; on average about four out of every five of his missions. In addition to the identification markings, like all the other Mustangs in the squadron, this aircraft has a yellow spinner and nose decking and a yellow rudder. The nose marking identifies the 361st Group and the rudder colour is for the squadron within the group. The two other squadrons which make up the 361st — the 374th and 375th Fighter Squadrons — have red and blue rudders respectively. Painted on the fin of Van's Mustang is the number 414685. This is the USAAF individual aircraft number, applied at the factory and based on the full aircraft serial number displayed in small characters on the left side of the fuselage below the windshield. There is only one number 414685 in the whole USAAF. Like many pilots, Van has bestowed personal insignia on the aircraft, for written in script below the exhaust manifolds is *Mary Mine*, a nickname in honour of his wife.

Lifting his parachute on to the wing, Van greets his crew chief, Sgt Sullivan. The sergeant knows better than to ask any details about the mission and confines his comments to: 'A long one today?' 'Yeah, looks like it', responds Van, and follows this with: 'How is she?' as he lights up a cigarette. 'Okay', Sullivan replies. 'She has a new set of spark plugs and runs

Below:
Carrying two 75 USgal drop tanks, *Duchess of Manhattan* awaits her pilot.

sweet. The radio man has changed those crystals and checked the VHF so you shouldn't have the crackling this trip.' 'Fine', acknowledges Van. 'We found a slight glycol leak near the fire wall', Sullivan continues, 'and had a hell of a job fixing it. Same place as before. I think we've gotten a slight kink in the knuckle pipe and I'm going to replace that first day the group's stood down.'

The discussion continues as they walk around the aircraft and Van gives it only a cursory inspection. He trusts Sullivan implicitly and does not want to do anything which might imply that he did not. Like all fighter pilots, Van knows that his very life depends upon the efficiency of his groundcrew. These men work long hours, often in appalling weather, to keep the aircraft serviceable and so a pilot should show appreciation and trust in this matter. This morning Sullivan and his assistant have been out on this exposed dispersal point pre-flighting the Mustang and ensuring all was ready for the task today, an hour before Van was awakened. A tent just off the hardstand is the only shelter that the two mechanics have against the elements. As Little Walden is perched on top of a hill, the ground personnel are frequently exposed to cold winds.

Seeing other pilots nearby climbing into their aircraft, Van decides that he too should get into the cockpit, but first a relieving pee — it will be a long flight and the relief tube is not the easiest of aids to use. A glance at his watch shows 09.40hrs and Engine Start is at 09.45hrs. Sullivan is on the wing and stretches out a hand to Van as he climbs up, using the left-hand main wheel as a step. Sullivan places the dinghy pack in the seat well and the parachute pack against the back rest. Van cocks a leg over the side of the cockpit, grabs the top of the windshield framing and levers himself into position, settling down on the seat. Now he goes into what has become a ritual: parachute and dinghy straps are secured around his person, then the quick-release safety seat straps fastened and pulled tight. In a crash-landing these prevent the pilot being thrown forward on to the instrument panel and the gunsight. The lead from the oxygen mask — which embodies the radio microphone — and helmet earphones is plugged into the appropriate jackpoint, the helmet having been donned before climbing on to the wing. Next, the oxygen mask hose is connected to the supply point and the regulators

turned to ensure the equipment is working. A quick glance that his belt-hung equipment is not in a position to hinder movement, and Van commences to check the aircraft's systems.

A cockpit check card is available but Van prefers to rely on memory and always makes a point of double checking everything. First he sees that the ignition switch is 'Off' and the fuel mixture control lever set at 'Idle Cut-Off'. Next, a look to see that the flap handle is in the 'Up' position and the carburettor air control lever forward on the 'Ram Air' mark. The three trim tab controls are set as the combat load demands. Landing gear handle in the 'Down' position, propeller control lever fully forward, throttle setting open an inch, gun safety switch 'Off' and gunsight switch 'On'. Altimeter adjusted to suit the 350ft elevation of the airfield and directional gyro uncaged. Rudder pedals and stick are then flexed to see there is no binding, with an eye on the actual surfaces to see they are responding correctly. Parking brake 'On'. Supercharger set to 'Auto' position, fuel shut-off valve turned 'On', fuel selector valve set for the left main tank; fuel booster, ignition, battery and generator switches 'On'. Finally, coolant and oil radiator doors are operated manually to ascertain if functioning properly and, when verified, the switches are set at 'Automatic'.

Having completed the cockpit check, Van signs the Form 1A that Sullivan has been holding, which covers the mechanical status of the aircraft. Its welfare has now passed from the crew chief to the pilot. The time is 09.43hrs, two minutes to Engine Start. Van stretches his arms; they are not cramped, it is simply a means of easing the tension that always seems to build in the minutes before starting engines. Each combat

mission is an adventure. There is no conscious apprehension about the flight ahead but a tightness often builds in the stomach while waiting. The dangers involved are accepted with a certain amount of nonchalance, each aerial warrior embued with the unspoken belief that it will be the other fellow who does not come back. The fighter pilot must be wise and aggressive. The cockpit of a Mustang is no place for a man consumed with his own welfare.

Suddenly earphones crackle with a message from the tower announcing that Engine Start is delayed. This can often happen when the bombers to be escorted are late in meeting their own formation assembly lines. Sometimes the delay is only a few minutes; on other occasions a half-hour or more. If the delay is substantial Van will cut all switches and get out of the aircraft for a stretch and another cigarette; he anticipates being confined in the cockpit for some four hours during the mission, so additional sitting time is to be avoided.

Sullivan, recognising his pilot's unease at this time, makes small talk, mostly about his experiences on a recent two-day pass to London. But the delay is short; the earphones crackle again; revised Engine Start is 09.50hrs. Sullivan slides down off the wing. As Van goes through the engine starting procedure he hears the splutter of a Merlin nearby as another pilot beats the clock. As Sullivan has already run the engine and it is warm, only a second's priming is required. The priming pump operating handle is on the bottom starboard side of the instrument panel and has a twist action lock. Van raises the protective cover over the switch and moves the starter to 'Start'. Immediately the electric motors whirr away and the propeller turns slowly in a clockwise direction (viewed from the cockpit).

After one revolution the engine suddenly fires, splutters and catches. With his left hand Van moves the Mixture Control lever against the throttle to 'Run'. This allows the automatic carburettor maximum fuel. The initial shudder and vibration as the engine started quickly subsides into a slight tremor of the airframe. A visual check of the oil pressure gauge shows it passing 60psi. Van lets the engine run up to just over 1,200rpm, watching the oil temperature and the suction gauge for the vacuum pump. The correct readings on the latter are important as this pump operates vital directional control instruments and also supplies the power to pressurise the two 75 USgal drop tanks attached to the underwing shackles. As all instruments show readings around the correct limits, the throttle is retarded slightly.

Sullivan is standing just in front of the left wing guns, in a position where he can easily see and be seen by the pilot. He holds a fire extinguisher in case there is a backfire and flames, although he knows this will be unlikely as Van never overprimes — the major cause of engine fires. Van raises a left hand, a signal for the wheel chocks to be removed. Sullivan acknowledges and pulls the chocks away from the left wheel while the assistant crew chief removes those from the right. Van raises his hand again to indicate he is about to release the brakes. Sullivan acknowledges and moves away from the aircraft but still keeps in a position where he can be seen from the cockpit. With the brakes off, Van gently eases the throttle forward and the Mustang begins to move. Sullivan has positioned the aircraft so that it is facing out towards the dispersal taxiway but Van needs to unlock the tail wheel and pivot the aircraft 30° so that he can watch his element leader's

aircraft, parked on a hardstand on the other side of the taxiway. Being a 'tail-dragger' the nose of the Mustang obscures forward vision. Other P-51s are moving past Van's on the taxiway and it is only a few seconds before E9:P, Van's element leader's identification, pulls out. As soon as this aircraft has gone by, Van applies some power and with a little right rudder swings out to follow. It is essential that the correct line-up is achieved now as there will be little room for manoeuvring for position when the head of the runway is reached. Once Mary Mine is headed down the taxiway the control column is returned from the fully forward to the neutral position. This locks the tail wheel although it still has 6° movement either way, sufficient to allow the weaving course necessary to keep the aircraft in front in view. Steering is achieved with the rudder, there being sufficient airflow from the propeller to allow control. It will only be necessary to push the stick right forward to unlock the tail wheel when making the sharp right turn into the perimeter track from the squadron's dispersal taxiway.

There is but a short distance to taxi to the head of runway One Zero which the 376th will use for take-off in an easterly direction. This will be the first squadron to depart. The second will be the 375th which is marshalling at the head of runway Zero Four. The 374th Squadron will marshal on One Zero while the 375th is taking off. In this way the time gap between each squadron take-off is kept to a minimum.

The mission leader, Capt Duncan, turns left on to runway One Zero and

Below:
Watching for the right moment to move on to the taxiway. Via D. Morris

taxis about 200yd along it before coming to a halt. His wingman pulls up on the left side of the runway, slightly behind the leader, and the other two P-51s that make up the other element of the lead flight position behind, staggered to the right of the first pair. The second element pilots are Walter Kozicki and George Vanden Heuvel. Van gently brakes Mary Mine to a standstill about an aircraft's length from the Group leader's Mustang. Other flights stack up behind the lead in similar fashion until all 16 P-51s of the squadron force are on the head of the runway.

Now each pilot runs through the pre-take-off check. To see that the ignition system is functioning properly, with brakes applied, Van runs up the engine to 2,300rpm and holds it there for about 10 seconds while each of the two magnetos is switched in and out to see if a drop in output occurs. If there is more than 100rpm drop, the ignition is not functioning efficiently. A final test for the magnetos is a quick flip off and on of the 'Off' switch. Sometimes low engine speeds while taxying can cause partial sooting of the plugs and it is then necessary to increase the manifold pressure to clear them. On this occasion both magnetos are within satisfactory limits. Next the constant-speed propeller is checked by speeding the engine to 2,300rpm again and moving the prop control lever to the 'Decrease' position. This brings the rpm shown on the tachometer back to under 2,000, indicating satisfactory functioning. Van returns the lever to full rpm and the speed returns to 2,300. The mechanical supercharger is tested by flipping the switch from 'Auto' to 'High' and the drop of 50rpm on the tachometer indicates this is satisfactory. Van then pushes the switch to 'Auto' and runs through a cockpit check of take-off settings: carburettor

air intake to 'Ram Air'; radiator shutter to 'Automatic'; oil cooler shutter to 'Automatic'; fuel booster pump to 'On' and a quick eye over the trim settings. Everything is in order.

Finally Van lowers his seat and then cranks a small handle on the right of the cockpit so that the canopy slides forward. He looks to see that the two red safety pins are located, indicating that the canopy is securely locked. The canopy is normally kept open while taxying to improve visibility from the cockpit; it also allows a hasty exit in an emergency. While tightening his seat harness (which had been kept loose while taxying) Van happens to glance in the rear-view mirror above the windshield framing and sees that a P-51 in the second flight has pulled off the runway on to the grass. Obviously it has some problem and is having to abort the mission. There will be a spare who will fill his slot in the formation after take-off; two spares are always scheduled for a mission.

Take-off signal usually comes from an Aldis lamp in the runway control vehicle that is parked just to the left of the runway in use. Today, with the prevailing wind in the northeast, this small, covered truck with its distinctive black and white chequerboard paintwork is at the head of Zero Four. The group leader with the 376th will rely on a radio message from the tower. Precisely on 09.56hrs it comes:

'Go Glowbright', which is the mission leader's callsign.

The first element is away. Van observes his element leader who is watching the first pair to see when they have travelled about two-thirds the length of the runway and are near the point of becoming airborne. The moment Kozicki's Mustang starts to move, Van's left hand advances the throttle lever to the position where he knows he will be drawing 61in of manifold pressure (forced boost into the intake manifold) and showing 3,000 engine rpm. A momentary glance at the instruments confirms this and he redirects his gaze through the right side of the canopy where the

runway edge can be seen over the wing. As *Mary Mine* picks up speed, the runway ahead is still obscured by the nose but it is wise practice to keep the tailwheel on the ground until at least 80mph indicated airspeed (IAS) has been reached. Raising the tail from the three-point position with the elevators before sufficient speed has

Below and right:
A squadron on the runway head awaiting the take-off signal. Wingmen take a position relative to that which they will assume once airborne — on the left or right of their element leader. Via D. Morris

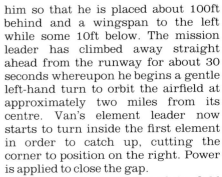

been built up can result in propeller torque, pulling the Mustang left. Van holds about 5° of right rudder to counteract any torque. Fully loaded with ammunition and fuel, including two external drop tanks, *Mary Mine* grosses near six tons and has covered a half-mile before the airspeed registers 80 IAS. Most of Van's attention is still forward over the right wing watching the runway edge, and with this as reference he gently eases the rudder pedals and keeps the Mustang straight up the runway.

The intersection with the northeast/southwest runway flashes by. Van gently pushes forward on the stick to bring the tail up, checks the airspeed again before applying back pressure on the stick and feels the main wheels leave the runway. *Mary Mine* is now airborne and the airfield threshold looms as Van drops his left hand from the throttle quadrant and pulls the landing gear lever smartly inwards and up. This is the critical time when a faltering engine can kill flying speed and make a crash or crash-landing inevitable. The exception perhaps, but it has happened to pilots of the group and at every fighter station in England. Happily, the Merlin is running true and strong and sustains *Mary Mine* up over the countryside. Van's attention has now focused on his element leader, turning in towards him so that he is placed about 100ft behind and a wingspan to the left while some 10ft below. The mission leader has climbed away straight ahead from the runway for about 30 seconds whereupon he begins a gentle left-hand turn to orbit the airfield at approximately two miles from its centre. Van's element leader now starts to turn inside the first element in order to catch up, cutting the corner to position on the right. Power is applied to close the gap.

By the time a half-orbit of the field has been completed, the first four-plane flight is in good position and the other three flights are in loose order, tightening turns inside the leaders to bring the whole squadron together. Van has now reduced the throttle setting to achieve 46in of boost and 2,000rpm for economical climb. By the time the group leader has completed an orbit of the field, all 376th flights are in position. The squadron consists of four 'finger-four' flight formations, so-called because the aircraft are staggered like the fingertips of a hand. Aircraft are also staggered down behind the leader so that his every movement can be followed. Likewise, every flight is stacked down behind the lead flight. Now 375th Squadron is in the air and 374th starting take-off. The group leader, who is also the squadron leader of the 376th, levels off at 500ft allowing the other squadrons to gain their position. Completing his second orbit, he crosses the field and sets course on a predetermined heading. It is now 10.09hrs.

The 375th Squadron is on the group leader's left and will eventually gain 1,000ft above the leading 376th as the group climbs towards the enemy coast. The third squadron, the 374th, is on the right about a mile away and flying approximately 1,000ft below the lead. Van, like all pilots in the formations, now switches from the left main internal fuel tank in the wings to the auxiliary fuselage tank. The vapour return vent line, which carries the vaporised fuel unused by the carburettor, runs to the left wing tank. It is essential there is sufficient space in the tank to receive the recovered fuel — which can be as much as 10 USgal in an hour — and for this reason the left main is always used to commence a flight. The fuselage tank holds a maximum 85USgal of fuel. When full, it adversely affects the handling of the Mustang through shifting the centre of gravity back to a point where it requires continual manipulation of the controls to maintain stability. In

Left:
A squadron sets course, flights stepped down and back from the lead.
Via D. Morris

13

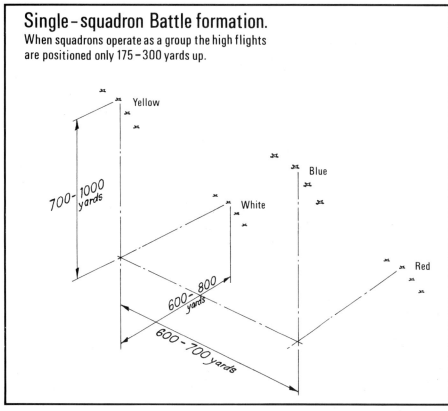

Single-squadron Battle formation.

When squadrons operate as a group the high flights are positioned only 175–300 yards up.

Yellow

Blue

White

Red

700–1000 yards

600–800 yards

600–700 yards

fact, trying to execute tight turns or pull-outs with a full fuselage tank has the effect of reversing the flight controls with dangerous consequences for the unwary. It is standing operational procedure during the climb-out to use the fuel in this tank first, reducing the contents to at least 25gal (and preferably more than this) and thus re-establishing the centre of gravity forward.

After changing tanks Van switches on the pitot tube heater. If the pitot system freezes up when higher altitudes are reached, there will be no air pressure to operate the airspeed indicator.

With the group on a direct course to its rendezvous point with the bombers, 450 miles away over Germany, it will be a case of follow the leader for the next hour. Fortunately the 361st

Above and right:
To avoid becoming separated when passing through cloud, pilots hold a tight flight formation on the climb-out. Once at high altitude each element spreads to give more relaxed piloting.
USAAF

14

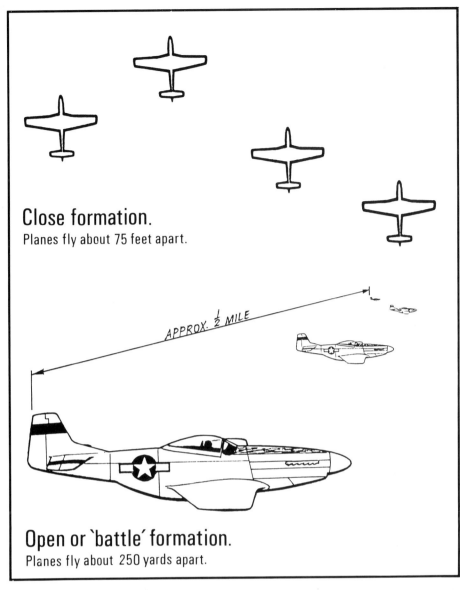

Close formation.
Planes fly about 75 feet apart.

APPROX. ½ MILE

Open or 'battle' formation.
Planes fly about 250 yards apart.

switch up to the 'On' position: the press trigger on the control stick hand-grip is now live. Far to the south another fighter group can be seen climbing towards the Continent, just specks in the distance.

The leader rocks his wings, a reminder to go on oxygen; the mask has been hanging free from Van's helmet. He now puts it in place and fastens it by means of a retaining clip, then moves the control lever on the oxygen regulator in the right-hand corner of the cockpit to 'Normal'. A blinker device on the regulator indicates a supply is being drawn. As with other American fighters, the oxygen system on the P-51 is a low-pressure demand type, which adjusts automatically to changing altitudes, furnishing the right amount of oxygen to the pilot. Oxygen bottles in the rear of the fuselage contain a sufficient supply for six hours' high-altitude flight. The formation is climbing at 160mph indicated. Economy is achieved by keeping the engine rpm low and adjusting the manifold pressure to achieve the desired speed. Low rpm precipitates plug sooting and every 15 minutes or so Van increases speed to 2,700rpm, holding it there for two minutes to clear the plugs.

At last through the haze a white line of surf marks the coast of Holland. Forty-five minutes from base they are about to enter hostile airspace. The radio crackles: 'Glowbright: Battle Formation.' This is the group leader's call for the squadrons and flights to spread out. The flight behind the lead increases power and fans out to the left to fly line abreast. The two trailing flights form a separate section of eight and veer to the right. Soon the 16 Mustangs are staggered in a line across a two-mile front, the second flights in each section flying about 50ft above and 50ft to the rear of the leads. At the same time, individual aircraft have separated from each other by about 250yd. The other two squadrons of the group are spaced out in a similar line on either side of the 376th so that the whole group force of 48 Mustangs advances on a front some nine miles in extent. This formation has been evolved as the best for making contact with the enemy, while being less vulnerable to surprise attacks and affording a wide canopy of protection for the bombers.

In addition to the group leader's call sign (Glowbright), each squadron has a call for radio communication. The 374th is 'Ambrose', the 375th 'Decoy' and the 376th 'Yorkshire'. The four flights of the squadron formations are identified as White, Red, Yellow and Blue, and the four aircraft within each flight as Leader, '2' (his wingman), '3' (leader of the second element) and '4' (second element wingman). This enables each member of the squadron to be identified and identify himself

Group does not have to climb through an overcast and, while some light cloud is forming at high altitude, visibility is good. The sun beats on the canopy and Van pulls down his tinted goggles to avoid having to squint.

The English coast north of Orfordness disappears below and the cold North Sea fills the downward view as the altimeter reads 7,000ft. In the past, a few pilots have had to bale out over the sea when their aircraft developed mechanical trouble. The Air-Sea Rescue service will go after you but there is little chance of survival unless plucked out very quickly. Such is the winter temperature of the sea that most men unfortunate enough to parachute into it quickly succumb to exposure.

Clear of England, Van reaches down and flips the gun and gun camera

15

over the radio without confusion as to his position. Today Van is flying Yorkshire White 4.

At just under 16,000ft there is a sudden surge of power from the engine, the supercharger blower has automatically changed into the high speed ratio. Van glances at the manifold pressure gauge which indicates a rise to more than 50in, but the needle returns to its original position as the manifold pressure regulator reacts to the supercharge input. Van has been taking occasional glances over his left shoulder at the gauge mounted on the rear fuselage fuel tank. It is now registering just under 25gal. He relaxes tension on the shoulder harness, reaches down in front of the stick and turns the fuel selector switch to the position marked 'Right Combat Drop Tank'. A distinct snap is felt as the valve is opened. There is an electrically driven fuel booster pump on each internal fuel tank to prevent vapour lock at high altitude and to ensure sufficient fuel supply to the engine-driven fuel pump whatever atmospheric and gravitational changes occur. The booster pumps also act as back-ups should the mechanical engine-driven pump fail as each alone provides sufficient pressure to feed the carburettor. There is no fuel gauge for the drop tanks and the first indication that fuel is exhausted in one or the other will be a dying engine. To avoid this, Van makes a mental note of the time, knowing the drop tanks will keep the engine supplied for at least two hours if required. From now on he will switch from one drop tank to the other around every 10 minutes to even the weight distribution and to improve handling characteristics.

The 361st is at 23,000ft as it passes north of The Hague and over the occupied Netherlands. As the climb progresses, the thinner air demands more pronounced movement of the stick and rudder pedals to affect the control surfaces, while uneven distribution of the load becomes more noticeable.

Despite the haze, landmarks on the western side of the Zuider Zee stand out in bold relief. Over towards Amsterdam a white trail lances vertically into the stratosphere: a 'Big Ben'. Van makes a mental note of the time as on return to base the Intelligence Officer will ask for Big Ben sightings. These are the awesome V-2 rockets. Only a quick glance can be spared for this spectacle as Yorkshire White 4 is now expected to keep a constant watch for any Bogies (unidentified aircraft) on his side of White flight.

'Glowbright to Decoy White Leader: you're pulling contrails.' Van looking out over his left wing to the north sees the distant shapes that are the 375th Squadron Mustangs trailing vapour, tell-tale signs that enemy fighters

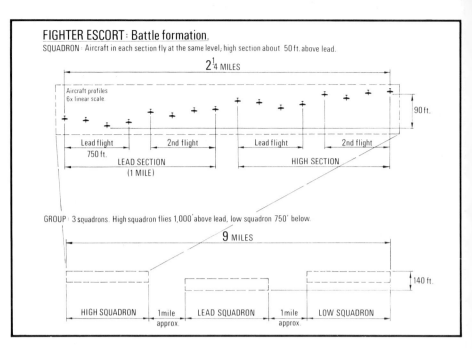

FIGHTER ESCORT: Battle formation.
SQUADRON: Aircraft in each section fly at the same level; high section about 50 ft. above lead.

2¼ MILES

Aircraft profiles 6x linear scale.

90 ft.

Lead flight | 2nd flight | Lead flight | 2nd flight
750 ft.
LEAD SECTION (1 MILE) | HIGH SECTION

GROUP: 3 squadrons. High squadron flies 1,000' above lead, low squadron 750' below.

9 MILES

140 ft.

HIGH SQUADRON | 1mile approx. | LEAD SQUADRON | 1mile approx. | LOW SQUADRON

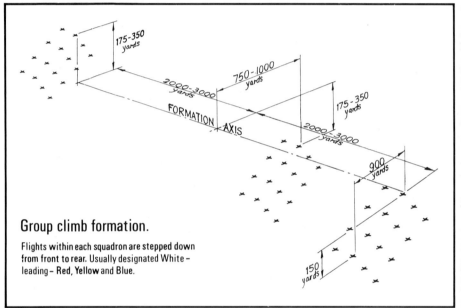

175-350 yards

750-1000 yards

2000-3000 yards

FORMATION AXIS

175-350 yards

2000-3000 yards

900 yards

150 yards

Group climb formation.

Flights within each squadron are stepped down from front to rear. Usually designated White – leading – Red, Yellow and Blue.

might spot. Within a few seconds Decoy White Leader and his followers have dropped down sufficiently to avoid the altitude band of freezing humidity where engine exhaust produces the contrail phenomenon. To maintain the height differential between squadrons, Yorkshire and Ambrose leaders reduce altitude by about 75ft.

Rendezvous with the bombers was scheduled over the Netherlands coast at 11.19hrs, but there is no sign of the Big Friends. They are either late or off course, Van muses.

The radio comes to life again: 'Decoy Blue 4 to Decoy Leader: Bogies 3 o'clock level — I think they are P-51s.'

'I see them. Let me know if they change course', comes the reply. Van looks to his right but cannot make out the aircraft in question. Most probably another escort group. He must not avert his gaze for long from searching the sky around him, twisting his head

to look back towards the rear. The mirror on top of the windshield covers too small an area of sky for this to be solely relied upon. Every other wingman is also searching the sky. Should some of the new enemy Me163 rocket or Me262 jet-propelled fighters come up to fight, spotting their approach is critical. Warned in good time, the flights can turn to meet an attack and minimise the chances of being hit. Head-on firing has little chance of finding its mark, such is the rate of closure.

'This is Glowbright. Can anyone see the Big Friends?' There is no response to the leader's call.

'Glowbright to Decoy: take your boys round to the north.'

'Roger, Glowbright', comes the response.

'Glowbright to Ambrose . . .' The rest of the radio message is drowned out by another, unintelligible radio call. Glowbright tries again: 'Ambrose, try south.'

'Roger, Glowbright.' Glowbright, alias Yorkshire White Leader, begins a gentle turn to the right. The rest of White Flight follows, as Van switches to another drop tank, checks his engine instruments and returns his gaze to the heavens. To his right he picks up specks that rapidly enlarge as he depresses the radio button on the end of the throttle lever to transmit: 'Yorkshire White 4 to Leader: Bogies 2 o'clock low.' By the end of this message the oncoming aircraft are clearly seen to be P-51s with white noses — the 355th Fighter Group, who were briefed to guard the second combat wing of B-24s. No one responds to Van's warning; the closeness of the passing makes this unnecessary.

Now Yorkshire earphones are filled with a high-pitched whine: for once the enemy has delayed his usual jamming noise. The whine is irritating but rarely impedes plane-to-plane radio communication.

'Yorkshire White Leader to Yorkshire White 3. I think I'm having trouble with C-Charlie. Will you take it? Repeat, will you take C-Charlie?'

'Roger, Yorkshire White Leader.'

The group leader is suspicious that the 'C' Channel frequency of his VHF radio set is faulty. This is the channel on which messages direct from bombers can be received. Glowbright is obviously concerned that he has been unable to contact the missing combat wing and suspects it might be radio trouble. As requested, Walter Kozicki presses the 'C' button on his VHF set and listens, but alternates between 'C' and 'A' channels so that he does not miss any further commands from Glowbright. 'A' channel also connects with transmissions from the fighter control centre in England via a relay aircraft over the North Sea. The two other channels, 'B' and 'D', are for calling for the Air-Sea Rescue and direction-finding homings, respectively.

Glowbright has now swept the Yorkshire squadron in a wide arc so that the unit is on a reciprocal course. Yorkshire White 4 is now on the extreme north of the flight formation instead of the south, an easier position to fly as he is not constantly looking into the sun.

'Ambrose Leader to Glowbright: our bombers 8 o'clock to you.'

'Roger, Ambrose Leader.' Glowbright continues his turn. Somebody, who does not identify himself, calls: 'There they are, ahead.' Through the haze the familiar shapes of Liberators appear, two groups in trail, about 60 aircraft. Yorkshire squadron turns over them at around 26,000ft; the bombers are at 22,000ft, just north of the Dutch town of Zwolle. It is 11.24hrs.

Now Glowbright accelerates and White and Red flights follow as their leader takes the section out some 10 miles ahead to intercept any attacks launched from that quarter. Yellow and Blue flights remain weaving above the bombers as close escort while the other squadrons protect each flank. Van switches fuel tanks again. As he does so there is a distinct 'crump'; a black smudge of smoke whips past over the right wing. Flak! Then, in quick succession, three red flashes down and away to the right, leaving more black markers that are quickly left behind. Yorkshire White Leader goes into a sharp left-hand turn to take the squadron away from

the barrage. Van automatically drops the nose of *Mary Mine* and banks left, passing under Number 3 to position on the other side of him as they come out of the turn. Number 3 has moved under White Leader and is now on his right, so that the positions of the other members of the flight are now reversed in relation to their leader, a move necessary to avoid disintegration of the flight in a tight turn. Yorkshire White Leader turns right and the members of this flight reverse the procedure to end up in their original positions as the course is resumed. The flak vanishes from the scene as quickly as it appeared.

A half-hour goes by. The bombers are approaching Wittengen, their IP (Initial Point) where they will turn for their run on the Misburg refinery. Van switches tanks again and tries to shift his position in the cockpit as his buttocks are uncomfortable. Fatigue threatens to sap concentration, but knowing the hostile environment in which he flies, there can be no slackening of lookout.

Suddenly the radio springs to life: 'Leader to all Glowbright aircraft; bandits at 9 o'clock low. Two large gaggles northeast of Ulzen.' At the same time Glowbright commences a diving turn to the left.

'Jeepers, look at them, there must be a couple of hundred', someone excitedly exclaims.

Van instantly drops his hand to switch the fuel selector to main tanks and then pulls the salvo handles just below the throttle control to jettison the drop tanks. Immediately there is a slight jump in airspeed and this quickly advances as Van pushes the throttle to the full open position in an effort to stay with White 3 who is diving to intercept the enemy hoard which appears to be making straight for the bombers. There are well over

100 single-engine fighters in mass formation and it is obvious that the eight Mustangs will be unable to deflect this force.

Van picks out an FW190 about 1,000ft below him, diving away. Pushing the throttle lever up to the stop, he attempts to overhaul the enemy who is increasing his angle of dive. Three or four seconds into the descent and Van feels a slight vibration in the stick. A quick look at the airspeed indicator shows the needle pointer climbing past 420mph which is over 530mph true airspeed at this altitude. Now the stick begins to resist Van's hand pressure and moves back and forth in a way he cannot control. As a result, the nose of the Mustang pitches up and down: compressibility — the phenomenon he has been told about but never before experienced. As the speed of the aircraft increases towards that of sound, so the flow of air over the wings is no longer smooth. Little is known about compressibility other than it will overstress an airframe and lead to its disintegration if not arrested. There is no time for alarm as the ground comes up towards the diving Mustang at a fearful rate. Van smartly chops the throttle to cut power. Still the Mustang heads down in a vice-like grip, resisting all attempts to move the stick. The altimeter unwinds rapidly: 15,000-14,000-13,000-12,000ft. At last, as the Mustang cuts into denser air some feel returns to the controls. Finally, around 10,000ft *Mary Mine's* nose starts to come up and presents her pilot with a horizon. Despite wearing a

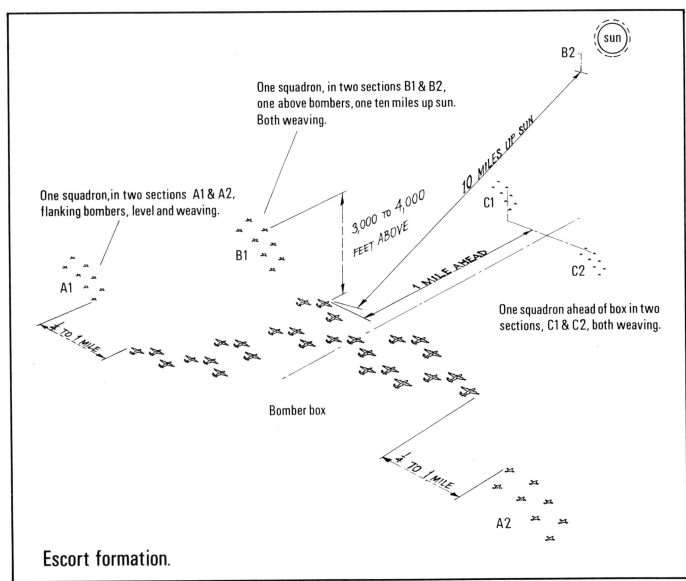

One squadron, in two sections B1 & B2, one above bombers, one ten miles up sun. Both weaving.

One squadron, in two sections A1 & A2, flanking bombers, level and weaving.

sun

B2

10 MILES UP SUN

3,000 TO 4,000 FEET ABOVE

1 MILE AHEAD

B1

C1

C2

One squadron ahead of box in two sections, C1 & C2, both weaving.

A1

¼ TO 1 MILE

Bomber box

¼ TO 1 MILE

A2

Escort formation.

Above:
A section some 4,000ft above curves over the bombers. This B-24J, *Hare Power*, was lost on the mission described. Via S. Gotts

Left:
The bombers attract the attention of flak batteries four miles below. USAAF

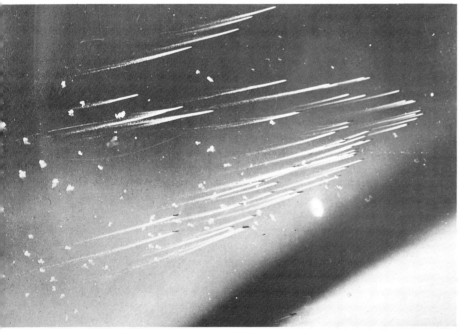

six diamond pips on the reflector plate match the wingspan of the FW190. He presses the trigger on the stick. Immediately he feels the Mustang yaw to the left. Van brings the fighter's nose back towards the target and fires again. Once more his aircraft skids left. He realises that only one of the six guns is working: there is no point in continuing the attack. White puffs of time-fused cannon shells alert him to break away. Even so, as he levels out in an attempt to run for it, Focke-Wulfs are seen coming in to attack from both flanks.

'Yorkshire aircraft break.' Van recognises Glowbright's voice in this warning.

Fear tightens the stomach, but his instant reaction to avoid the cannon shells and bullets that will be unleashed at *Mary Mine* in a fraction of a second is an abrupt left forward movement of the stick. The Mustang slices over and down into a Split-S (a roll over into a dive, reversing direction of travel). A glance upwards and Van is amazed to see both of his antagonists disintegrating in flames: one that had been closing in on *Mary Mine* in an inverted position had slammed into the other. Speeding down away from the debris of this

G-suit, the stress on Van's body is such that he momentarily 'blacks out'. Spots pass before his eyes. He looks at the altimeter and sees he has dropped from 26,000ft to recover at 9,000ft. Only now does shock take its effect: the body exudes perspiration in protest. As his head clears, Van swings round to see if the enemy are present. The sky is clear but for heavy contrails away to the south.

Opening the throttle, Van climbs towards these, curving in a wide spiral to try and keep a true airspeed in excess of 250mph. Being alone, it is necessary to keep a constant lookout for a surprise attack from above. As 19,000ft is reached, aircraft are seen

approaching at roughly the same altitude from the east. As a precaution, *Mary Mine* is levelled out and turned in towards them. A wise move, for the aircraft are soon identified as FW190s at *Staffel* strength — a dozen or more. Alarmed at the situation in which he now finds himself, Van pushes the throttle 'through the gate', breaking the safety wire to gain emergency power, and calls for assistance over the radio: 'This is Yorkshire White 4. I need help. Angels 17. South of Ulzen.'

Turning in behind one of the Focke-Wulfs, Van frames the enemy in the K-14 computing gunsight, adjusting the throttle grip until the collision, Van is careful not to let the airspeed build up and take him into compressibility again. Twisting his head, he makes sure none of the other FW190s are following him down.

Relieved to find himself alone again, Van once more recovers to a higher altitude along the bomber track. At 22,000ft specks ahead become single-engine aircraft: he has run into more FW190s manoeuvring to attack a distant group of B-24s. In the hope of dispersing the enemy, Van turns in behind one. His intended victim flies on a steady course, apparently un-aware of the danger coming up behind. The K-14 sight range pips are adjusted and the instant the Focke-Wulf's wingspan meets the circle they form, Van presses the gun trigger. Once more only a single weapon fires pulling the P-51's nose left. Dismayed that five guns still will not fire, Van promptly decides to disengage before he again becomes a target for the enemy. Diving away to use the momentum to gain high altitude, Van realises he has neglected to survey the instrument panel during the combat. The engine coolant and oil tempera-ture gauges both show readings in excess of the permissible maximum — past the red warning lines. Alarmed, Van realises that he still has the throttle right forward in the War Emergency Power position and quickly retards it. War Emergency Power (WEP) had been drawn off and on for 30min instead of the maximum of five. He checks the setting of the radiator scoop doors for maximum cooling but these are already fully open.

'This is Glowbright, assemble south of Hanover at escort angels'. The 361st leader is trying to bring his scattered group together. Van is not sure of his position as his Mustang flies west. Unable to locate his group rendezvous and with no sign of friendly aircraft, the prudent action is to call for a homing. He presses the fourth button on the radio to communicate on Channel 'D' and calls:

'This is Yorkshire 56. I require a QTM. Yorkshire 56. Give me a QTM. 4 . . . 3 . . . 2 . . . 1 . . .'

After a few seconds comes a distant response: 'We have you Yorkshire 56. Steer two-seven-oh. Repeat: Yorkshire 56, steer 270. You are 180 miles.'

'Roger, loud and clear. Thanks', Van responds. He is further west than he thought.

When not checking the instruments and remaining alert for enemy 'bounces', Van takes the occasional squint at the ground far below. After a few minutes he makes out the shape of the Zuider Zee. Then out to the right he sees a yellow-nosed, yellow-tailed Mustang sliding in towards him. The 376th pilot waggles his wings and the markings E9:D identify the newcomer as Glowbright — John Duncan. Van

Above:
A pursued FW190 drops its auxiliary fuel tank and takes evasive action.
USAAF

takes up position to fly as his Number 2. It is a relief to have company. Evidently the 376th became so scattered during combat that the leader was unable to rally a formation.

Duncan makes radio contact: 'Yorkshire L-Love. I'm making for Manager. My pills are low.'

'Roger, Yorkshire White Leader. I'll tag along', is Van's response. The message tells him that the other pilot's fuel supply is diminishing and that he is going to land at the Allied forward base of A-92 St Trond in Belgium to refuel.

Mary Mine's oil temperature gauge has dropped back to 78°C and the coolant has come down to 110°C much to Van's relief, but the engine is still running far from smoothly. Van presses the transmit button: 'Yorkshire White 4 to Yorkshire Leader. My engine is running rough so I don't want to push it any more than 40 inches.' There is a delay and then Van catches 'Okay' and a few indistinct words. Somebody else is transmitting on the same frequency at this time.

'Will you repeat, Yorkshire White Leader.' The identification Van now

uses is for Duncan as the squadron leader instead of group leader.

'Roger White 4. I'll hold it down.'

'Thanks', responds Van. The fuel gauges in *Mary Mine* show a total of 53gal, just sufficient for the estimated 45min flight back to Little Walden, but it is prudent to refuel at St Trond in case the weather deteriorates, forcing a longer flight time than anticipated. Some B-17s appear off to the left and then the sea comes into view ahead; the two Mustangs are now clear of hostile airspace.

'Yorkshire White 4: I'm going over on to "D" to call for a homing.'

'Roger', Van replies. The earphones sit easier on the ears now as the radio jamming noise has ceased. He pushes button 'D' to go over to that channel in time to hear Duncan call: 'Hello Manager, Hello Manager. Give me a QTM. This is Yorkshire Two Zero. Give me a QTM. 4 . . . 3 . . . 2 . . . 1 . . .'

A British voice responds: 'Roger Yorkshire 20, steer one nine zero. Repeat, steer 190.'

'Roger, Manager.' The reverse count by Yorkshire 20 allows the direction-finding radio station to obtain a directional bearing, thus enabling them to issue a heading to fly. In calling for homings or the Air-Sea Rescue, pilots use a personal number-in-group identification.

Yorkshire White Leader goes into a shallow bank and levels out to obtain his heading while Yorkshire White 4 follows. With enemy-held territory left behind the gun switch is turned off and Van can relax from the constant head-turning. However, he is not one of the many pilots who wear a silk parachute scarf round the collar to prevent the chafing of the neck that can result from two hours twisting to and fro. *Mary Mine* is beginning to overrun the leader so Van takes the throttle back a little and then a little more as Yorkshire Leader begins to lose altitude more rapidly. When the altimeter needle drops below 10,000ft Van closes the oxygen regulator valve and unclips the oppressive, sweaty mask. Now, almost instinctively, he changes hands on the stick, edges off his left glove, and extracts a cigarette from the packet of Chesterfields in his right breast pocket. Matches follow, to be held with the stick hand while the right extracts the match, strikes it and lights up. Smoking in the cockpit is not officially condoned but most fighter pilots do it on letting down from altitude.

Five minutes later, when down to 4,000ft, Van looks to see Duncan rocking his wings and giving the thumbs down sign. Van rolls his aircraft to port and sees an airfield. They have reached Manager, alias St Trond.

Button 'D' is pushed on the radio for airfield-to-plane communication. Yorkshire Leader has just transmitted but Van only catches the end of his message. Then Manager Tower comes back with: 'We have you Yorkshire Leader. Use runway 19. There's a C-47 on approach and a B-17 next. Orbit until I give you the okay.'

'Roger, Manager', Duncan replies. They go into a left-hand circle round the field. Visibility is improved but high cloud is starting to build up at around 10,000ft. As they sweep round, Van carries out landing preliminaries. The right main tank has 20gal of fuel in it and he switches to this and sees that the booster pump switch is on. He then stubs out the cigarette and flips it into the ash can before tugging at his safety harness to ensure it is tight. Completing an orbit of the airfield, Van notices the B-17 touching down and a moment later the tower calls: 'Yorkshire 20 and Number 2, come on in.'

'Roger, Manager.' Duncan banks and Van follows to come in parallel to the runway in use, diving slightly and maintaining a speed of just over 210 IAS. Three-quarters of the way down, Duncan pulls up and peels off left. Van continues along the line of the runway for about two seconds before pulling back on the stick to follow, up and round about a quarter-mile behind the leader. Turning in for final approach about a mile outside the perimeter of the airfield, Van brings back the throttle lever until the IAS drops

below 175. He then reaches down with his left hand and moves the landing gear lever down and into the 'Locked' position. As the wheels drop, the nose of the Mustang pitches down a little. It takes more than 10 seconds for the gear to extend and lock in, during which time Van adjusts the elevator trim tabs to compensate for the nose heaviness. A squint at the landing gear indicator lights at the bottom of the instrument panel shows that both main wheels are down and locked. The engine is still running unevenly and Van keeps the speed at 170 IAS as he curves round behind Yorkshire Leader.

Above:
Joining up for the flight home.
D. Morris

About three-quarters of a mile out, Van turns *Mary Mine* into the final approach, shifting the flap lever when the airspeed drops past 165 IAS. Like the main landing gear, the flaps take from 10 to 12 seconds to fully extend. Normally Van would let the speed drop away to 120 IAS as the flaps slow the aircraft, but with the rough-running engine he feels it wiser to keep the throttle further up the quadrant and the speed to 140. Lining up on the centre of the runway, Van brings *Mary Mine* down at a slightly higher angle than normal and not until the threshold of the runway does he reduce power to let the IAS slip under 120mph. The engine splutters as he lets the tail come down a little. The engine misses again and flying speed drops off quite fast, although Van now has *Mary Mine* in a three-point position and only a few feet above the runway surface. Within another five seconds the main wheels touch and the tailwheel follows around two seconds later. There is the distinctive thump as the weight of the aircraft settles on its oleos. Van keeps the stick back and the tailwheel locked and lets the Mustang run the length of the runway diminishing speed.

Turning left on to the perimeter track, his first action is to unlock and slide back the cockpit canopy. The fresh air is welcome. Yorkshire Leader has been directed by a 'Follow Me' jeep into a Pierced Steel Plank (PSP) standing about 200yd along the track. The jeep with the sign pulls off to one side. Van pushes forward on the stick to unlock the tailwheel and swings round beside E9:D. He holds *Mary Mine* on the brakes and runs the engine up to 2,000rpm. At high revolution the engine runs reasonably smoothly but as soon as the throttle is brought back it misfires. John Duncan is already out of his aircraft and is giving instructions to the control jeep driver for fuel. Van catches Duncan's attention by waving and pointing to the engine of *Mary Mine*. Duncan walks over and listens as Van runs the engine up to some 40in of boost. The Merlin is certainly not performing smoothly and after a few moments Duncan draws his hand across his throat — the 'cut' sign. Van pushes the propeller control fully forward, action which makes for easier starting next time. The throttle lever is moved back until the engine is idling at 1,550rpm before turning off the fuel booster pump. The fuel mixture control lever is moved to the 'Idle Cut-Off' position and, as the rpm drops off to below 600, he gently opens the throttle to clear the carburettor. Finally, he cuts the ignition and all other electrical switches before closing the carburettor air intake shutter to the filtered air position to keep out blown grit. In case the brakes have overheated during taxying, the parking lever is not applied to avoid discs seizing.

Radio, G-suit and oxygen supply connections are unplugged and seat straps cast off for a very stiff Van to hoist himself up, holding on to the windshield frame. Four hours and 22 minutes have given him a sore rear end and stiff muscles. He pulls off his helmet and goggles and rests them on the dinghy pack; it is a relief to be rid of the incessant noise. Cocking a leg over the cockpit side, Van gets on to the wing, walks back and jumps off. It is good to stretch. Van goes over to discuss the mission. Both men are eager to get home to Little Walden to discover how the group fared. It has been a long time since the 361st had contact with the enemy on such a scale and the two pilots speculate that it may be one of the most successful days of air fighting. Both light up cigarettes while Van relates how gun stoppages cheated him of a possible victory. He also learns that Duncan witnessed the collision between the two FW190s following Van's smart evasive action.

A fuel tanker moves in and after checking that Purple Peril (150 octane aviation spirit) is required, the crews start to refuel the Mustangs. Van

borrows a tool and gets up on the wing of *Mary Mine* to unlatch the gun bay doors. The cause of the jamming appears to be misaligned trace links preventing the ammunition from feeding into the gun breaches properly. Van curses his armourer although he is not sure of the exact problem or who is at fault. This adds to his determination to fly home this day. An Engineering Officer arrives: he has heard *Mary Mine's* spluttering engine as it taxied in and suggests the aircraft remain for examination and a spark plug change. Van has no desire to spend a night at A-92 and says the engine is okay when under load. The Engineering Officer voices his disapproval and Duncan agrees with him. Van is to stay the night at St Trond while his leader will take off for Little Walden as soon as his P-51 has been refuelled.

The engineering officer gives Van a ride to his billet and promises to arrange for a mechanic to look at *Mary Mine's* engine first thing in the morning. An adjacent mess hall provides refreshment where other 361st Group pilots are present, having also come into St Trond because of battle damage or mechanical problems. There is, however, no one from the 376th.

After a restless night, punctuated with the passage of V-1 flying bombs overhead, Van rises early to ensure the engineering section gets to work on *Mary Mine*. Even so, it is 09.00hrs before a mechanic can be spared. After the cowling access panels have been removed, several broken spark plug leads are found and replacements gleaned from a wrecked P-51 nearby. Some of the plugs are also changed. The engine is started up for a test but still runs unevenly, although better than the previous afternoon. The

Engineering Officer advises leaving the Mustang at St Trond and returning to England by transport aircraft. But Van is anxious to have his base armament officer check the inoperative guns to see if the armourer was at fault.

After some discussion, Van obtains permission to taxi the Mustang to another area and pull full power from the engine. After three minutes at 3,000rpm he considers the engine is running smoother so radios the Manager Control Tower for permission to take-off for a short test flight. The tower responds: 'Clear to roll Yorkshire. Left-hand circuit around the field taxiway. Wait for the control jeep and follow him.'

Nearly two minutes elapse before the 'Follow Me'-placarded jeep comes into view and positions for the P-51 to follow. During this time Van has been concerned about the coolant temperature which has risen near to the red line. He is relieved to see this drop when finally moving out on to the taxiway again. While weaving along the track Van notes that some of the taxiways still have unfilled bomb craters; it would certainly be unwise to have moved without following the control jeep. St Trond is a large airfield but there is only a short distance to travel to reach the runway in use. Van goes through the pre-take-off check and lowers 15° of flap to improve lift before he commences his run. The engine vibrates and is noisier than usual but responds well and Van does not draw excessive power in the climb-out. He circles the airfield, gradually gaining height, taking some 20 minutes to reach 18,000ft.

If the engine continues to function reasonably well the intention is to fly back to England. Having carefully monitored the instruments and found

everything satisfactory, the decision is taken to head for Little Walden. First, permission must be obtained from Manager Control and Van contacts them over the radio. The response is affirmative with the instruction to call Bluefrock (the emergency direction-finding station at Manston) to ensure they are aware of the flight. Van acknowledges, heads west, calls Bluefrock and is given a bearing heading. He maintains a high altitude until well over the Channel in case the engine falters and also to avoid inviting warning fire from anti-aircraft artillery as he crosses in. The British defences were likely to consider anything below 8,000ft over the Channel area as hostile although, in practice, they realise that battle-tired pilots may be forgetful and some damaged aircraft cannot maintain high altitude, so only a warning shot is fired. As an added safeguard, Van flips a switch on the right side of the cockpit which brings his IFF (Identification Friend or Foe) set into operation. This set, emitting a distinctive pulse signal via a small antenna under the rear fuselage, identifies the aircraft as friendly to a receiving Allied station.

Cloud starts to build up as the Channel comes into view. Although his engine appears to be running satisfactorily, Van takes the precaution of going over to the Air-Sea Rescue channel periodically to see what radio traffic it carries should the worst occur. The crossing takes only six minutes before the distinctive shape of North Foreland, the point on the north Kent coast leading into the Thames and London, comes into view. Van banks right, changing the radio to the homing frequency and seeking Little Walden.

'Hello Darkfold, Hello Darkfold. This is Yorkshire 56, Yorkshire 56 give me a QTM.' He has to repeat his call twice before Darkfold responds and gives him a new heading. Visibility is fair and he drops down to around 3,000ft. The sprawl of London can be seen to the west. There is no need for another homing call as Van can now navigate by reference to landmarks that are clearly seen. The town of Chelmsford looms to the right ahead and he alters course to the northwest. *Mary Mine* passes over two or three airfields that are in use by RAF transports and then, off to the left, the 4th Fighter Group's home at Debden shows up — the red-nosed Mustangs dotted around the field confirm this location. Next airfield up the line is Little Walden.

As the home field comes into view Van calls Darkfold for clearance to

land and receives an affirmative. He sees many hardstandings are empty: the group is out on another mission. A shallow dive parallel with the runway and peel off into curve round to land, follows. As Van reduces engine power there is a pronounced splutter and misfiring so he keeps a good turn of speed on final approach. Lining up for his touchdown he sees he is in risk of catching up with another P-51 landing ahead. There is nothing for it but to go around again.

The throttle is advanced to give 46in manifold pressure reading while applying right rudder to counteract the left-hand swing brought about by engine torque. A quick movement and the landing gear handle is brought back to the 'Up' position. Van waits for the tail-heaviness that will become

Above:
A breath of fresh air after several hours' confinement in the cockpit. USAAF

apparent as the gear comes up, requiring elevator trim. *Mary Mine* begins to pick up speed as Van edges up the flaps while keeping the stick forward to resist the nosing-up tendency that develops. When the airspeed has picked up to 170, Van feels relief. If the engine had spluttered at the critical point, a stall might have resulted. Even now Van keeps the Mustang headed out from the runway in a straight course and only when the IAS shows near 200 does he begin a left-hand circuit for another approach.

This time things go smoothly and he makes a reasonable three-pointer, knowing that Sullivan and a lot of other groundcrew men will be watching. It is important to be seen to be a good and careful pilot.

After landing it takes several minutes to taxi round the perimeter track to the 376th dispersal area. When Van eventually returns *Mary Mine* into Sullivan's hardstand, the crew chief and his assistant are waiting. Another P-51 shares the loop-type concrete hardstanding so it is necessary for Van to unlock the tailwheel, apply one brake and gently pivot *Mary Mine* round to face out to the taxiway. Sullivan stands where his pilot can see him and uses hand signals to direct Van. As the switches are cut and the Merlin splutters into silence, the assistant crew chief places wheel chocks and Sullivan hops up on to the wing. Sullivan is concerned about the sound of the engine. Van is more concerned that his guns jammed. Sullivan has the Form I on which he enters all the mechanical problems encountered by Van. The armourer joins Sullivan on the wing and after listening to Van's complaints moves across to open the weapons bay and inspects the guns.

Left:
Capt John Duncan, 376th Squadron Operations Officer. Below the map on the instrument shroud is a packet of Wrigley's gum! Via S. Gotts

Ground crew inspect *Mary Mine's* engine.

Five minutes elapse before Van initials the Form I and hauls himself out of the cockpit. It coincides with the arrival of a jeep that has come out to take him to the Squadron Ready-Room. It is driven by another pilot who calls for Van to hurry up and some banter issues between the two pilots as Van lugs his parachute pack off the wing and stows it in the back of the jeep. When the jeep departs, Sullivan and his assistant have decided to replace the spark plugs and change the oil before giving the engine a test run. If it isn't satisfactory they intend to have the Line Chief and the Engineering Officer come out and decide if an engine change should be made. The armourer is starting to remove the guns for transport to the armoury for examination. There will be at least two hours' work repairing and replenishing *Mary Mine* for her next flight. If the test runs on the

engine are not satisfactory and a change is in order, it may mean an all-night shift for the hangar crew of the service squadron.

The jeep takes Van to the group briefing room. On entry the pilot is greeted by the S-2 Officer (Intelligence), who jokingly complains about his late arrival through stealing a night on the town in Belgium. The orderly brings coffee and doughnuts while the S-2 sits down with Van and takes his report. Van learns that, as

suspected, the 361st Group has had its best day's air fighting ever, with tentative claims of 23 enemy aircraft shot down for one loss. Most of the enemy aircraft destroyed were the heavily-armoured FW190s of an assault group caught while attacking the B-24s. His intelligence reports given, the pilot is transported to his quarters where, after freshening up, he will go to the Officers' Club to join other pilots in talking over details of yesterday's successful mission.

Below:
Servicing Browning M2s in an armament shack, a necessary task after every mission. L. Nitschke

MISSION SUMMARY REPORT.

MISSION SUMMARY REPORT.

PRIORITY
TO BE TRANSMITTED BY OI TELETYPE./CONFIDENTIAL, IN THE CLEAR.
TIME OF ORIGIN -   DATE - 26 -- 11 -- 44.
ORIGINATED BY - Maj. Ellis   AUTHORIZED BY - Maj. Ellis

FROM: OIHAK

TO : OISFW
      OIPNT (ATT DIR OF INT DUTY OFCR)
      IAH (ATT DIO AEAF BATTLE ROOM)
      OIKHI
      OIAWW

A. 361ST FIGHTER GROUP _____ FLYING.
B. 48 P51S (374th-19; 375th-16; 376th-13) UP 1009 DOWN 1447.
C. 5.
D. PENETRATION, TGT & W/D SUPT 1ST CW 2ND FORCE 2BD FC NO. 529B.
E. 2 P51s - 1 P51 DUE ROUGH ENGINE (PILOT BAILED OUT ████
      WALCHEREN IS.) 1 P51, REASON UNKNOWN.

F. 1 P51 CAT "AC" DUE CRASH LANDING BURY ST.EDMUNDS (PILOT SAFE).
G. 2 (SEE PAR E.)

H. 19-0-9 SE AIR.

I. R/V'D 1ST CW 2ND FORCE 1124 JUST N ZWOLLE 22,000 FT. BOMBERS APPROX
    5 MINS LATE. FORMATIONS FAIR. ENCOUNTERED 350/400 PLUS FW190S/ME109S
    IN 3 WAVES 15 MI S ULZEN & JUST W WITTINGEN AS BOMBERS APPROACHED IP.
    COMBAT ENSUED FOR 45 MINS (SEE PAR. L. BELOW) FOLLOWING WHICH, DUE
    ENDURANCE, ONLY 1 FLT WAS ABLE CONTINUE ESCORT, PICKING UP 2 SMALL BOXE
    RED TAIL 96TH CW B24S AREA S DUMMERLAKE 1250 & ESCORTING TO DUTCH/GERMA
    BORDER W LINGEN WHERE W/D ████. 355TH GP OBSERVED IN COMBAT AREA &
    56TH GP IN TGT AREA.   1320

J. NIL.
K. OBSERVATIONS: 1-- ROCKETS: 4 BIG BENS, 1 PINPOINTED 4VY9505 1040.
    OTHERS FROM VIC AMSTERDAM 1050, 1340, 1350. 5 BIG
    BENS FROM VIC THE HAGUE 1057, 1335, 1400, 1340, 135
    2 █ BIG BENS FROM VIC ENSCHEDE 1240, VIC ROTTERDAM 12
    2-- 1 P51 DOWN IN FLAMES WITH 1 WING OFF 20 MI E TGT. NO CHUTE.
    3-- 1 P51 DOWN VIC 15 MI W HAMELN 1245. 3 CHUTES SEEN THIS AREA.
    4-- 3 B24S DOWN TGT AREA 1235. TOO FAR AWAY TO SEE ANY CHUTES.
    5-- 1 B24 EXPLODED AS LEFT TGT. NO CHUTES SEEN.
    6-- 1 P51 DOWNED BY E/A 1235 AREA OF CELLE. PILOT BAILED OUT & LANDED IN
        WOODS.
    7-- 50/100 CONTRAILS HEADING W FROM VICINITY CELLE 30,000 FT 1230.
    8-- 2 FW190S SEEN TO CRASH HEAD-ON DURING COMBAT (PAR. I. AND L.).

L. GP ENCOUNTERED 3 WAVES FW190S/ME109S TOTALLING 350/400 VIC S ULZEN
    & WITTINGEN. AT 1210 1ST WAVE OF APPROX 200 APPROACHED HEAD-ON FROM
    EAST WITH MAIN GAGGLE AT 23/24,000 FT & TOP COVER AT 28/29,000 FT.
    376TH SQ ATTACKED & SMALL GAGGLE THESE E/A BROKE FORMATION THE
    AT THE BOMBERS. REMAINDER CONTINUED FLYING HELL BENT WEST & DID NOT GET
    RETALIATE WHILE AT THE BOMBERS. CLAIM 6-0-1.
    AT 1215 2ND WAVE COMPOSED OF 3 GAGGLES FW190S/ME109S TOTALLING 60 AT
    23,000 FT WITH AN ADDITIONAL 20 PROVIDING TOP COVER AT 30,000 FT
    APPROACHED FROM NORTH & AWAY FROM ████████ SUN IN 4-SHIP LINE
    ABREAST FORMATION. 375TH SQ ATTACKED & CLAIM ____ 8-0-3
    THESE E/A WERE VERY AGGRESSIVE & IT IS BELIEVED JERRY PLANNED THIS GAGGLE
    TO ENGAGE FIGHTERS TO PAVE WAY FOR 1ST _____ WAVE OF 100 E/A PASSED
    UNMOLESTED. ALSO DURING THIS _____

MISSION SUMMARY REPORT.

MISSION SUMMARY REPORT.

PRIORITY
TO BE TRANSMITTED BY OI TELETYPE./CONFIDENTIAL, IN THE CLEAR.
TIME OF ORIGIN -   DATE -
ORIGINATED BY -   AUTHORIZED BY -

FROM: OIHAK

TO :

A. 361ST FIGHTER GROUP.

                    PAGE -- 2 --

    OVER AND HIT THE BOMBERS.
    AT 1220 JUST EAST OF IP NEAR WITTINGEN ANOTHER WAVE OF 60 PLUS
    FW190S/ME109S AT 20,000 FT APPROACHED FROM EAST & HEADED FOR
    BOMBERS. 374TH SQ ATTACKED, DISPERSED & CLAIM 5-0-5.

M. NIL.
N. NIL.
O. NIL.

                    --- end ---

SEPARATE MESSAGE:

FROM: OIHAK

TO : OISFW

A. 361ST FIGHTER GROUP.

P-1. 8 NYPS: 6 DOWN A-92, 1 UNREPORTED, 1 BAILED OUT.
     LT DIXON & LT T. MOORE, 374TH SQ, A-92.
     LT. WOOD, LT. FARNEY, F/O HART, 374TH SQ, A-92.
     LT. VANDEN HEUVEL, 376TH SQ, A-92.
     LT. W. R. STEVENS, 375TH SQ, A-92.
     LT. H. R. AUTH, 375TH SQ., UNREPORTED.

P-2. 19-0-█ S/E AIR.

374th Sq. 5-0-5		375th Sq. 8-0-█.3.		376th Sq. 6-0-1	
1-0-0 FW190 MAJ GLESSNER		2-0-0 FW190S CAPT NEELY		1-0-0 FW190 Lt.	
1-0-1 FW190 LT. WILKERSON		1-0-0 ME109 LT SULLIVAN			Kozicki
1-0-1 FW190 LT. HICKS		1-0-0 ME109 LT ADAMS		1-0-0 FW190 Lt.	
0-0-1 FW190 CAPT LACROIX		1-0-0 ME109 LT KLEES			Chadwick
1-0-1 FW190 LT CHANDLER		1-0-0 FW190 LT TRAVIS		2-0-0 FW190S █ Capt.	
1-0-1 FW190 LT VEAR		1-0-0 ME109 LT MCCOPPIN			Beyer
		0-0-2 FW190S LT SPAULDING		1-0-0 FW190 Lt.Ford	
		0-0-1 FW190 LT FARNUM		1-0-1 FW190s Lt.Scott	

Above:
**Group Mission Summary Report, copies
of which were sent to Wing, 8th Air
Force, AEAF Headquarters, Division
and US Strategic Air Forces.**

Right:
**George Vanden Heuvel's combat
report.**   G. Vanden Heuvel

Below:
**Lt George Vanden Heuvel, a
photograph taken on return from the
mission described.**

COMBAT REPORT

A. Combat
B. 26 November 1944 F.O. 529B 2BD
C. 376th Fighter Squadron
D. 1300
E. 15 mi S/Ulzen
F. Air to Air Good
    Air to Grd Good
G. FW 190's
H. 2 FW 190's destroyed

I. I was flying Yorkshire white Four - Escorting B-24's.
    We were about 15 miles south of Ulzen when 50 plus FW
    190's approached the bombers from the east. We broke
    into them and I got into a dive at 500 plus mph and
    could not pull out until I was at 10000 feet at which
    time I was alone. I climbed up southwest along the
    bomber track looking for some one to join up with.
    I was at about 20000 when I saw 10 plus FW 190's ahead
    and they broke into me. I turned into them and man-
    euvered onto a FW's tail. I fired a burst and after
    the first few rounds only one gun was firing. I saw
    no hits, while I was on this FW 190's tail several
    other FW's were making side passes at me but scored
    no hits on me. Two FW 190's, coming from about opposite
    sides, were closing in and shot from about a 80 degree
    deflection angle. I dumped the stick and made a steep
    diving turn. The two FW 190's collided almost head -
    on and exploded and fell in a flaming mass. I continu-
    ed on out of that area. I claim 2 FW 190's destroyed.

J. 410 rds expended
A. C. E94 44-14625

George R. Vanden Heuvel
GEORGE R. VANDEN HEUVEL,
1st Lt., Air Corps.

(1) Dest air
(2) Dest air

DECLASSIFIED
E.O. 11652, Sec. 3(E) and 5(D) or (E)
945.005
NARS, Date 7/24/75

2
Combat Evaluation

A number of qualified observers have adjudged the North American P-51 Mustang the best all-round fighter aircraft of World War 2. While acknowledging that the type had a good performance, equal or better in most respects to that of its contemporaries, this accolade undoubtedly owes much to the aircraft's actual combat achievements. Mustangs, primarily in the squadrons controlled by the US 8th Air Force, played the leading role in establishing air superiority over the Luftwaffe during the spring of 1944, and then maintaining this ascendancy to the end of hostilities in Europe. The type eventually predominated in the USAAF fighter units operating against Japanese forces, where it achieved considerable success. Although the Mustang had originally been designed to a British order, RAF and Commonwealth air forces, not having a major escort fighter requirement, had a lower priority for their supply of Merlin Mustangs.

Largely as a result of 'popular' presentation by the news media, the Mustang has been labelled a war-winning aeroplane and hung with the myth of having superlative qualities. Thereby the public has been conditioned to accept a dog-fighting view of air combat. But the advantages that one high-performance fighter type had over another were of far less importance in aerial warfare than the way in which these aircraft were employed. The fixed machine gun or cannon armament and the overall performance limitations of the subsonic piston-engined aircraft of the period dictated the basic tenets of air fighting, where the advantage of altitude was utilised to attack and recover. One of the most successful and experienced pilots has said that in his estimation the majority of the fighter pilots shot down never saw the enemy aircraft that was responsible. In other words, surprise had been the crucial element. The combat manoeuvring that supposedly epitomised air fighting in World War 1 was, in World War 2 more the exception than the rule — particularly in the later stages.

In exploiting surprise and evading enemy reaction, a high diving speed was of paramount importance. In fact, aircraft with otherwise relatively poor performances in comparison to their adversaries — for example the Curtiss P-40 — were used with some success by exploiting their ability to pick up

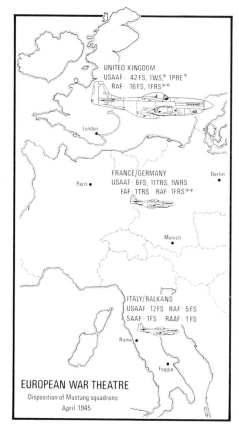

EUROPEAN WAR THEATRE
Disposition of Mustang squadrons
April 1945

UNITED KINGDOM
USAAF: 42 FS, 1 WS,* 1 PRE*
RAF: 16 FS, 1 FRS**

FRANCE/GERMANY
USAAF: 6 FS, 11 TRS, 1 WRS
FAF: 1 TRS RAF: 1 FRS**

ITALY/BALKANS
USAAF: 12 FS RAF: 5 FS
SAAF: 1 FS RAAF: 1 FS

London
Paris
Berlin
Munich
Rome
Foggia

PACIFIC WAR THEATRE
Disposition of Mustang squadrons
August 1945

IWO JIMA
USAAF: 9 FS

RYUKYU ISLANDS
USAAF: 7 FS, 2 TRS, 2 ACS

CHINA
USAAF: 11 FS, 1 TRS

BURMA
USAAF: 1 TRS

Tokyo
Peking
Shanghai
Chungking
Hong Kong
Saigon
Rangoon

speed in a dive. The ability to out-dive an opponent was possibly the most advantageous factor in World War 2 fighter performance where attack from altitude, recovery and escape was the usual tactic.

The P-51 could overhaul and out-dive practically all its combat contemporaries and attain speeds that took it into the realms of compressibility.

This was attributed to good streamlining and presenting a relatively small frontal area, but mostly to the so-called laminar flow aerofoil of the wing. In contrast to most wing aerofoils of the day, which had the thickest section towards the leading edge, the laminar flow aerofoil had the thickest point further back, allowing less initial disruption of air flow.

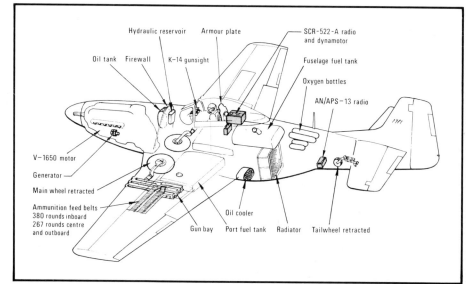

Hydraulic reservoir   Armour plate   SCR-522-A radio and dynamotor
Oil tank   Firewall   K-14 gunsight   Fuselage fuel tank
Oxygen bottles
AN/APS-13 radio
V-1650 motor
Generator
Main wheel retracted
Ammunition feed belts
380 rounds inboard
267 rounds centre
and outboard
Gun bay   Port fuel tank   Radiator   Tailwheel retracted
Oil cooler

P-51B Merlin-engined Mustang's instruments were 'red-lined' at 505mph IAS as maximum safe diving speed; beyond this the airframe would be under excessive strain. Some eager pilots, trying to overhaul a fleeing jet, neglected to watch the instruments and speeds well in excess of this limit occurred. The airspeed instrument was operated by air pressure through a pitot head. As the density of air varies with altitude, so the reading of the instrument varied from true speed. A true speed of 500mph was only 300mph indicated at 30,000ft. At 20,000ft it was 400mph IAS. At 10,000ft — 480mph IAS, and not until descent reached 5,000ft did the IAS approximate to true air speed. The warning of excess speed came through stiffening controls, a slight pitching up and down of the nose and tail buffeting. A feature of such high speed dives in Merlin Mustangs, particularly those with a fuselage fuel tank, was the phenomenon of stick reversal forces which, unless understood and correctly countered by the pilot, could precipitate loading forces on wings and tail during the attempt at recovery that could cause them to fail. Even so, many an uncautioned pilot took his Mustang into compressibility and survived to report that his aircraft had suffered nothing more than 'a few popped rivets'.

Merlin Mustangs normally required only light pressure of the stick to operate the controls, and in combat situations unguarded handling or the use of very sharp manoeuvres could put considerable strain on the structure. This was particularly so when the introduction of the G-suit allowed much sharper turns and pull-outs in that it prevented a pilot suffering 'blackout'. Previously, the risk of 'blacking out' had a restraining effect on pilots who were then less inclined to be hard on the flight controls. In short, such was the ease of handling the Mustang that it lent itself to pilot abuse. Equally, it allowed advantages in attack and evasion that were decisive. While the Mustang airframe was a reasonably robust design, it did not have the reserve of structural integrity that, for example, the P-47 Thunderbolt had. While specific structural weaknesses were highlighted and dealt with by modification and other means, throughout its period of operational use there were frequent cases of Mustangs being lost through structural failure — at one time estimated as at least two per week in the European Theatre of Operations. Of those where the exact cause could be identified, there was often no common factor. Overall, these losses appear to have been through general structural strain brought about by uninhibited piloting.

The original Allison-engined Mustang had been designed with a maximum all-up combat weight of 8,000lb; the structure was sufficiently robust to withstand any gravitational strain likely to be induced by pilot action through the flight controls. The change to the heavier and more powerful Merlin and its allied accessories increased the weight by some 1,200lb over the earlier model. This combination of extra weight and power challenged the original design limitations and introduced some undesirable characteristics. Most notably directional stability which, in the Allison-powered version had been good, was deemed poor in the early Merlin Mustangs, requiring constant rudder pedal vigilance when not trimmed out to counter the torque of the powerful engine and four-bladed propeller. In some flight situations the aircraft was prone to side-slip and, if not countered, a snap roll or spin out could quickly follow. Poor directional stability was even more pronounced in the first P-51D and K models with their cut-down rear fuselage deckings. The addition of a small dorsal fin, and changes in the operation of the rudder trim tab, were soon introduced to restore directional stability and overcome the tendency of the aircraft to veer off on its own into stressful flight attitudes.

Taking-off in most high-powered single-engined fighters required pilot vigilance with directional control, and in the Merlin Mustang this was particularly so. Many unwary newcomers to the cockpit of a Mustang were alarmed to find the aircraft veering off the runway to the left. This was most noticeable with pilots transitioning from the docile P-38 Lightning with its contra-rotating propellers. There were a number of fatal accidents in these circumstances where pilots completely lost control of a veering Mustang.

In contrast to the Allison-powered version, more cautious handling became necessary with the introduction of the Merlin engine, caused primarily by the attendant weight and power increases.

The matter was compounded by the addition of an 85 USgal fuselage fuel tank. As mentioned on page 16, when full this tank moved the centre of gravity aft, making the aircraft longitudinally unstable.

With experience, pilots learned the limits to manoeuvring that could be undertaken while a large amount of fuel remained in this tank. Forward pressure on the stick during turns helped to counter the misplaced centre of gravity.

During production of the Merlin-engined Mustangs, several design improvements were incorporated to strengthen wings and tailplanes to withstand the extra stresses highlighted by failures in operational use.

Below:
The basic component of a fighter formation was the two-plane element — leader and wingman. A good wingman never lost contact with his leader and maintained a 200 to 300yd separation in hostile airspace — a distance judged by being able to read the identity letters on the leader's aircraft. USAAF

Above:
Formation flying demanded a constant eye on the leader with head turned in his direction, particularly when flying close. The Merlin Mustang's propensity to veer from the course when power changes were made could bring trouble for the inattentive pilot. S. Evans

While these went some way to reducing instances of structural failure, there was still plenty of scope for over-eager pilots to exploit the speed and manoeuvrability inherent in the design. In fact, nothing short of a complete redesign to allow for high or gravitational forces could eliminate the problem. Better structural integrity, coupled with a lighter airframe, were the combined goals of later P-51 projects, notably the P-51H which appeared too late to enter war service.

While the Mustang's performance may have rated as good or better than most contemporary piston-engined fighters, its armament left much to be desired. The first Merlin Mustangs, the P-51B and C models, had only four 0.50in calibre machine guns. Two additional guns enhanced the firepower of the P-51D and K models, but

Below:
Because of the high nose attitude of the Merlin Mustang the pilot's view ahead was severely restricted when taxying. While this did not impose much difficulty when negotiating concrete perimeter tracks with defined limits, it was a different matter in open field conditions. To ease the pilot's lot when taxying and positioning, most units operating from field landing grounds had a crew chief ride on the left wing to act as a guide. These 354th Group P-51Bs assembling at Lashenden, England, for a sweep over France, all have wing guides.
Smithsonian Institution 59175AC

Above:
The fatal result of loss of directional control: this P-51D veered off the runway during take-off at Honington, severed the tail of a parked B-17, and ended up a flaming wreck.

it still took an accurate concentration of hits on an enemy aircraft to cause its destruction. A pursuing attack from the rear was the more likely to provide an opportunity to register the desired concentration, range being of paramount importance. The wing-mounted guns had to be harmonised so that their fire would converge at a certain distance, normally 300yd; although the setting used depended on unit policy and individual preference. In deflection shooting — opening fire when attacker and target aircraft flight paths converge — demanded skill and a certain amount of good fortune to obtain a 'kill'. Even accurately-made deflection shots might register only two or three bullet strikes on the target because of a fleeting moment when range was correct.

The original armament of four Browning machine guns together unleashed 50 rounds/sec. In practice, long bursts were required to bring sufficient hits to destroy an enemy fighter. The six guns of the P-51D and K improved the rate of fire to 75 rounds/sec. Regardless of model and armament, most Mustang victories were achieved through a strike igniting the enemy's fuel or ammunition, leading to explosion or fire. Although the average concentration of strikes was much higher with machine guns

than with cannon, the destruction caused to the airframe was usually considerably less. While the destructive power of a single 0.50 bullet was not to be underestimated, its chance of inflicting crippling damage to the enemy aircraft was not high. In fact, a postwar survey concluded that only the armour-piercing incendiary round had proved lethal through its combined penetration and inflamatory capabilities. The chief weakness of the 20mm cannon, used extensively in British, German and Japanese fighter armament, was a much slower rate of

fire — around two-thirds the rate of a 0.50 calibre machine gun. Later German weapons not only had better rates of fire but larger explosive charges so that a single hit was often sufficient to render crucial damage and precipitate destruction of the fighter targeted.

The positioning of guns on Mustang wing mountings could be adjusted to harmonise the weapons for the desired point of range convergence. They could also be elevated or depressed from the aircraft's flightline. For air combat the guns were elevated 2°

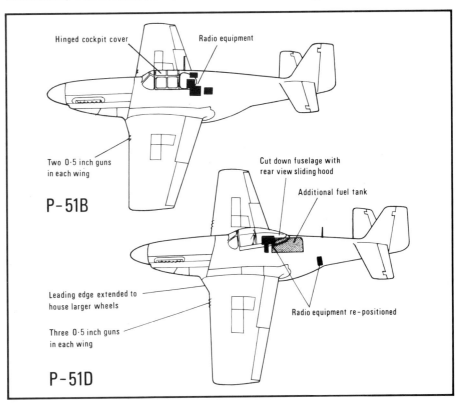

Hinged cockpit cover
Radio equipment
Two 0·5 inch guns in each wing
P-51B

Cut down fuselage with rear view sliding hood
Additional fuel tank
Leading edge extended to house larger wheels
Radio equipment re-positioned
Three 0·5 inch guns in each wing
P-51D

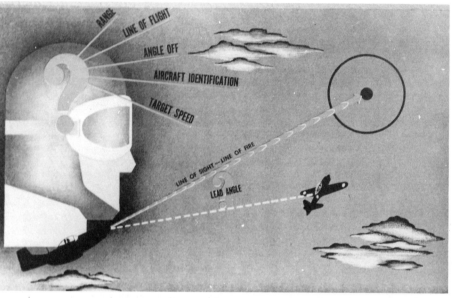

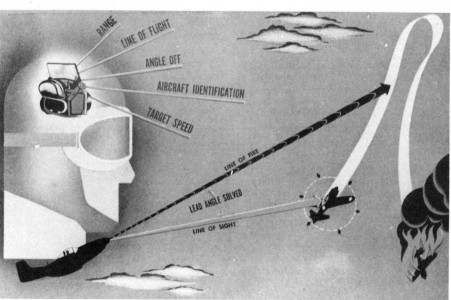

Left and centre left:
On the P-51B and earlier models the outer 'Point Fifties' were set lower in the wing so that all guns were on the same horizontal plane. In the P-51D all three guns were positioned along the line of the wing leading edge. Maximum ammunition stowage in the 'D' was 1,880 rounds, 620 more than in the 'B'. USAAF

above the normal flight attitude at cruising speeds to give the maximum amount of sighting over the nose at a target aircraft. For ground strafing it was the practice in many USAAF units to set the guns parallel with the aircraft datum line.

The Mustang was a good gun platform in so far as firing had little effect on the stability of the aircraft. The P-51B and C models (Mustang III) had convoluted feed from the ammunition bays to the guns, which initially produced serious problems with jamming rounds. This was found to be due to the gravitational pull on the ammunition trace when firing occurred during fast manoeuvres, a feature of most fighter-fighter combat. Modifications and a powered trace feed reduced the incidences of gun jamming in the P-51B and C while the redesign of the ammunition feed for the P-51D and K further improved the situation. Nevertheless, the ease with which involuntary manoeuvres could be affected with the Mustang and the very high G-forces induced, would still occasionally result in rounds jamming.

The P-51B and C retained the same cockpit canopy design as the earlier Mustangs. While it allowed reasonably good forward and down vision

Below:
The so-called gyroscopic gunsight was not readily accepted by many experienced fighter pilots. To 'sell' the benefits of the new sight, which revolutionised deflection shooting, this poster was issued to USAAF P-51 units. The sight was capable of computing a lead angle ranging from 200 to 800yd. Via I. Mactaggart

Above:
Based on a British design, the K-14 gyroscopic gunsight—being far bulkier than the N-9 reflector sight it replaced — proved difficult to install in a Mustang. One of the neatest arrangements was carried out on 357th Fighter Group aircraft and subsequently refined and adopted by many other units converting to the K-14. Note the crash-pad to prevent injury to the pilot's face. M. Olmsted

around the aircraft's nose — better than the contemporary Spitfires and Bf109s — it left much to be desired in general all-round visibility. In the USAAF it was held in contempt by pilots as the 'Coffin Hood'. The RAF gradually equipped all their squadron service Mustang IIIs with a one-piece blown bulging canopy known as the Malcolm hood, similar to that fitted to the later Spitfires. The conversion programme was slow as the single production source could not meet the demand and because runners had to be fitted so that the hood could be slid back over the rear fuselage fairing; this in turn requiring the repositioning of the radio mast. The Malcolm hood provided a great improvement in visibility, particularly to rear quarters, and was popular with both RAF and USAAF pilots. The P-51D (Mustang IV) introduced the bubble canopy which gave a pilot 360° all-round vision above the horizontal plane. As recounted above, the reduction in rear fuselage decking that came with this new canopy had an effect on directional stability.

Before the installation of a fin extension, constant pilot attention was required on the rudder pedal to counteract engine torque. Although the bubble canopy was acclaimed for the vastly improved all-round view from the cockpit, there was still a need for rear-view mirrors attached to the windshield fairing. These were invaluable when a pilot was concentrating on attack in that they allowed momentary shift of sight to see if another enemy was positioning at the rear. Such was the pace of combat that turning one's head to search the rear might find the quarry ahead gone when eyes were again brought to the front. The introduction of the AN/APS-13 tail warning radar during the final months of hostilities provided

a useful aid in avoiding surprise attack from the rear. Mustangs fitted with this device could be visually identified by the small antenna projecting on both sides of the tail fin.

At maximum permissible power, 3,000rpm and 67in mercury indicated manifold pressure — which equated to plus 18lb/sq in in the British system of measuring boost into the engine — the P-51B and C attained an average maximum speed of 435mph at 30,000ft. Variation between individual aircraft was notable, particularly those with highly polished wing surfaces as against well-worn examples where wings were deeply scratched, scored and dented. This could make more than 5mph difference, all other things being equal. The projecting wing pylon racks were estimated as costing 10mph at high speed and two full 108 USgal drop tanks took 40mph off the maximum.

The original Merlin Mustangs were fitted with the V-1650-3 model engine. With the V-1650-7 series, fitted to later production, the best speed was obtained at 25,000ft, supercharger

Below:
Armament personnel of 355th Fighter Group discuss the gun problems of the P-51B. The angled site of the two guns and the convoluted feedways can be clearly seen in this photograph.
USAAF

Above:

Mustangs which 'bellied in' after an engine failure were often worthy of repair. Apart from the propeller blades, the radiator housing took most of the impact, the scoop having a braking effect on soft ground. Pilots could usually walk away from wheels-up landings as in the case of this 505th Fighter Squadron P-51B in May 1944. However, the airframe was not salvaged due to main spar distortion. USAAF

THE CANOPY

CANOPY CRANK AND EMERGENCY RELEASE INSIDE

The cockpit enclosure is of the half-teardrop type; it consists of an armor glass windshield and a sliding canopy formed from a single piece of transparent plastic. The canopy is designed to give you the best possible vision in all directions, since obstructions above, at the sides, and to the rear have been eliminated.

You get into the cockpit from the left side. To help you up on the wing, there is a handhold in the left side of the fuselage. You can step on the fairing in getting up on the wing, but be careful that you **don't** step on the flaps.

To open the canopy from the outside, push in on the spring-loaded button at the right forward side of the canopy, and slide the canopy aft.

You control the canopy from within by means of a hand crank. Depressing the latch control on the crank handle unlocks the canopy, after which you can turn the crank to slide the canopy open or closed. Releasing the latch control locks the canopy in any position.

To warn you against taking off without having the canopy properly secured to the airplane, there are two red indicator pins, one at each side of the canopy. If these pins are visible the canopy isn't properly locked.

Never take off if you can see the pins. If you do, your canopy will blow off.

EMERGENCY RELEASE INDICATOR

The emergency release for the canopy is the long red handle on your right, above the oxygen controls. When you pull this handle, the entire canopy flies off. The handle is safetied with light safety wire.

ratios having been changed to produce better power output at lower altitudes.

Both the P-51D and K were approximately 300lb heavier than the B and C models, mainly accounted for in the additional armament and ammunition. While the top speed in level flight was only slightly less — an average 430mph — climb to high altitude for similarly matched examples took a good minute more for the D and K models. In combat this was not particularly noticeable as most climbs were preceded by dives which afforded momentum. Despite the heavier wing loading, the P-51D and K still handled well in combat manoeuvres. Many pilots with experience of both B and D preferred the former for the extra performance edge. However, most did not hesitate to trade the performance and handling advantages for the extra firepower and outstanding cockpit visibility of the later models.

Illustration from Pilot Training Manual for the Mustang

Facing page:

Contrast in profile between two P-51Bs, one with the original three-section hinged canopy, the other with the sliding Malcolm hood, and the P-51D with 'teardrop' canopy.
USAAF/G. H. Weckbacker

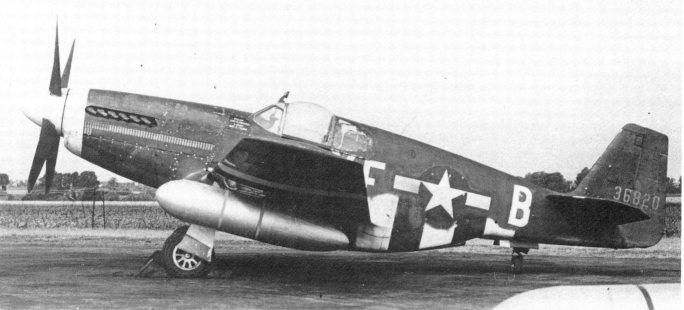

3
Combat Comparison With Contemporaries

The performance differences between the various model Merlin Mustangs is comparatively insignificant in operational terms and the same may be said of the German types met in combat — the Messerschmitt Bf109 and Focke-Wulfe FW190. Only in the last few months of hostilities were versions of these German fighters in production with substantially improved performances and a few were met in combat. The Japanese fighters encounterd by USAAF fighters in the Pacific and Far East war zones were of more varied types and performances. Broadly speaking, the Merlin Mustang was superior or equal to all its German piston-engined contemporaries except in the rate of climb. Against the best of the Japanese fighters, the same held true, but additionally Japanese fighters had better turning ability than the Mustang. The climb deficiency was due to weight rather than power, a loaded P-51D averaged 10,500lb, an FW190A 9,000lb, a Bf109 7,000lb and a 'Zero' 6,000lb.

A number of comparison tests were run with the Merlin Mustang against other contemporary fighter types by both the Allies and the Axis. Fighter pilots with experience in other types also carried out individual evaluations. The following is based on a consensus of findings.

Level Speed
At 25,000ft the Merlin Mustang was an average 35mph faster than the Bf109G, 50mph faster than the FW190A, 90mph faster than the Mitsubishi A6M5 'Zero', and 60mph faster than the Nakajima Ki84 'Frank'. In comparison with the British and US contemporaries the Merlin Mustang was 25mph faster than the Spitfire IX, 15mph faster than the Tempest V, 20mph faster than the P-38J Lightning and about 5mph over the P-47D and F4U Corsair.

Reducing to the lower altitude of 10,000ft, the P-51B and P-51D were approximately 25mph faster than the Bf109, 50mph faster than the FW190A, 80mph faster than the 'Zero', and 60mph faster than the 'Frank'. Against Allied types the Mustang still had a 15-20mph advantage over the Spitfire IX, P-38J, P-47D,

F-4U, while the Tempest V was about 15-20mph faster.

Climbs
In a sustained climb at full power the Bf109G gradually outclimbed the Merlin Mustang but this was less marked above 20,000ft. In 'zoom climb' (a climb preceded by a dive to gain momentum) there was little to choose between performances. In a climb to altitude against the FW190A, the enemy type had a slight advantage. In zoom climbs the Mustang was the faster. From a level start the Mustang could outclimb both the 'Zero' and the 'Frank' although these lighter aircraft had better initial acceleration. The Spitfire IX outclimbed the Merlin Mustang at all altitudes, while the Tempest and Corsair could better it only below 10,000ft. The Mustang had a slightly better rate than the Lightning but the Thunderbolt was left far behind.

Exploiting a zoom climb the Mustang could surpass all these types in climbing acceleration. The P-47 could match it initially but decelerated rapidly.

Dives
A Mustang diving could pull away from, or overhaul, the four enemy types so far mentioned. However, this was less marked against the Bf109 and a prolonged dive was necessary to achieve a safe separation. Spitfires were easily out-dived, as was the P-38J, due to the latter's limitations on diving speed. The Tempest and Thunderbolt could stay with the P-51 Mustang although it had better initial acceleration and could often maintain separation.

Turning Circles
The Mustang could easily out-turn the Bf109G, but in this respect had little advantage with the FW190A. However, the FW190 had a tendency to suddenly drop out if turned too tightly. Against the Japanese fighters the Mustang was at a disadvantage for both the 'Zero' and 'Frank' could quickly and easily turn inside a P-51. Compared with Allied types the Mustang could out-turn the Tempest, Thunderbolt and Lightning, while the

Spitfire easily turned inside the Mustang's tightest effort.

Rate of Roll
Ability to revolve a fighter around its longitudinal axis was particularly advantageous in evading enemy attack as it allowed quick entry into a dive. The Mustang's rate of roll was similar to that of the Bf109, but inferior to the FW190's. Compared to the Japanese fighters, the Mustang tended to have a slower rate of roll at slow speeds and lower altitudes, the position improving as speed increased towards 400mph. This was also true in comparison with the Spitfire IX but the Mustang was much faster in rolling than the Tempest or Lightning. Surprisingly, for such a large aircraft, the P-47's rate of roll was better than the Mustang's.

In actual combat, initial speeds and altitudes were major factors in determining how one type would perform against another. Turning fights much depended upon the skill of the individual pilots in handling their aircraft. Good use was made of the Mustang's ability to enter high speed skids, both in evading and positioning for attack. Even with the knowledge that his aircraft was superior to the enemy type engaged in combat, a prudent pilot did not rely on this supposed advantage. As mentioned above, the performance and flight characteristics of individual aircraft varied considerably. There might not be a 50mph speed advantage over the opposing Bf109 or the ability to turn with it and gain advantage. Nevertheless, some general recommendations were given by the Allied air forces for combat with Mustangs. Against the Luftwaffe's 109s and 190s, turning and climbing fights were not desirable and not to be entered into at less than 200mph indicated air speed. Turning, climbing fights with Japanese single-seaters were to be avoided at all times. The advised method of engaging Axis fighters was dive and recover, maintaining a high speed at all times. Indeed this came to be the hallmark of Allied fighter tactics during the period when the Mustang was operated, a technique known as 'strike and recover' or 'hit and run'.

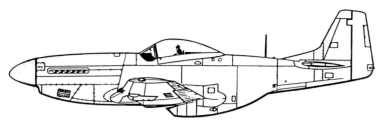

P-51D Mustang

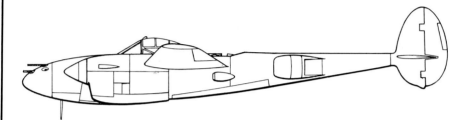

P-38J Lightning

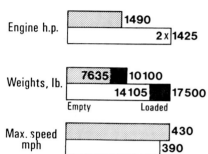

Engine h.p. 1490 / 2 x 1425

Weights, lb. 7635 10100 / 14105 17500
Empty Loaded

Max. speed mph 430 / 390

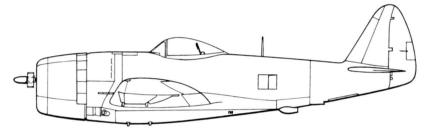

P-47D Thunderbolt

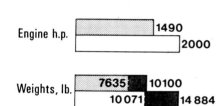

Engine h.p. 1490 / 2000

Weights, lb. 7635 10100 / 10071 14884

Max. speed mph 430 / 429

Engine h.p. 1490 / 1520

Weights, lb. 7635 10100 / 5850 7600

Max. speed mph 430 / 402

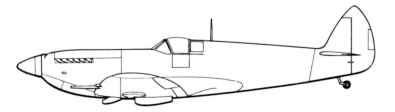

Spitfire F. Mk IXᴇ

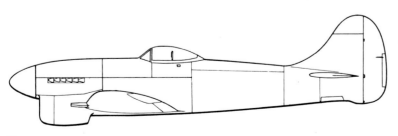

Tempest F. Mk V

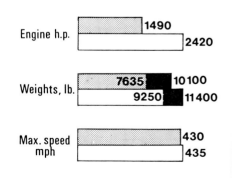

Engine h.p. 1490 / 2420

Weights, lb. 7635 10100 / 9250 11400

Max. speed mph 430 / 435

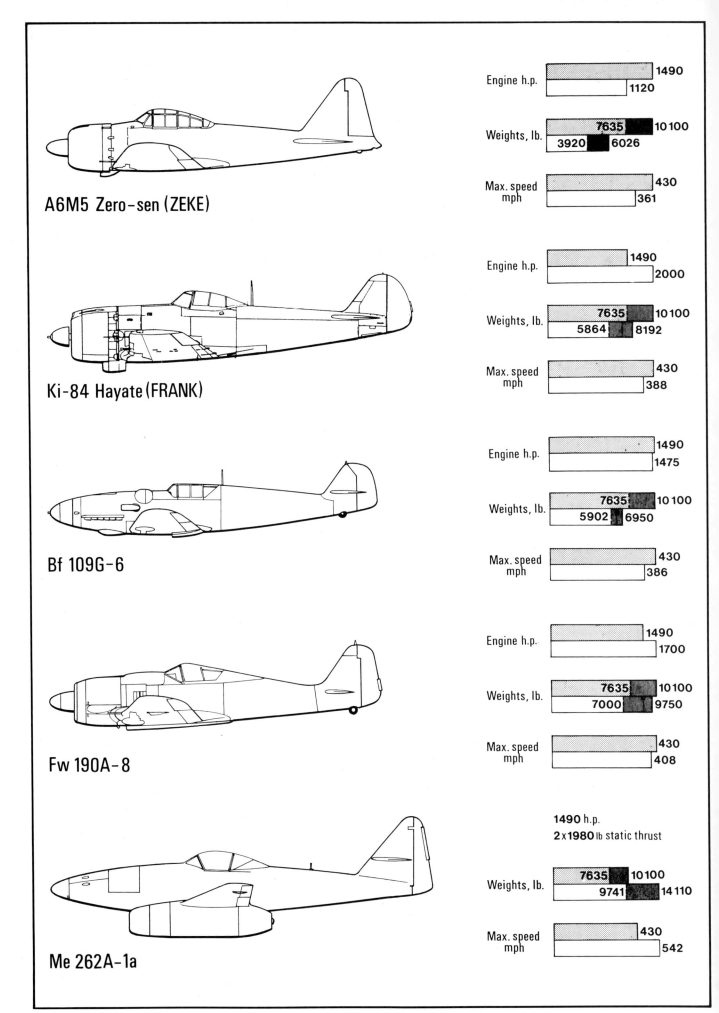

A6M5 Zero-sen (ZEKE)

Engine h.p. 1490 / 1120

Weights, lb. 7635 / 10100 — 3920 / 6026

Max. speed mph 430 / 361

Ki-84 Hayate (FRANK)

Engine h.p. 1490 / 2000

Weights, lb. 7635 / 10100 — 5864 / 8192

Max. speed mph 430 / 388

Bf 109G-6

Engine h.p. 1490 / 1475

Weights, lb. 7635 / 10100 — 5902 / 6950

Max. speed mph 430 / 386

Fw 190A-8

Engine h.p. 1490 / 1700

Weights, lb. 7635 / 10100 — 7000 / 9750

Max. speed mph 430 / 408

Me 262A-1a

1490 h.p.
2 x 1980 lb static thrust

Weights, lb. 7635 / 10100 — 9741 / 14110

Max. speed mph 430 / 542

For defence when attacked, Mustangs turned to meet their assailants head-on. Turning to meet the attacker usually spoilt his aim and deflected the attack. In cases where the attacked were outnumbered it might not be possible to turn in time to meet every assailant. Then the only evasive measure for a Mustang pilot was to dive away, barrel-rolling and skidding if a pursuer was too close behind. Rarely could a Mustang fail to evade in a dive. Conversely, when the Mustang was the pursuer, a lucky Bf109 might escape by diving, but rarely so; an FW190 had little chance as did both Japanese types. Overall the most significant factor of the Mustang's success in air fighting lay primarily in its diving ability.

The only enemy aircraft that challenged the P-51's supremacy was the Messerschmitt Me262 jet. Fortunately this was never available in sufficient numbers to pose a real threat to Allied air superiority and the type was also beset with mechanical problems. The only Allied jet available — in much smaller numbers — was the Gloster Meteor, which had a comparable performance, possibly more reliable engines, but an inferior airframe to the Me262. Furthermore the Meteor, like the Me262 and other early jets, had a high fuel consumption and so a very limited endurance. A Meteor squadron based in Holland during the final weeks of the war never made contact with enemy jet aircraft.

Although the first P-51D Mustang versus Me262 combats occurred in the autumn of 1944, the incidence of jet encounters did not reach significant proportions until early in 1945. By this time the weaknesses of their operation had been identified, in particular their short endurance — an average of 40 minutes. Mustang units of the US 8th and 15th Air Forces were briefed to loiter in the area of known Me262 bases and endeavour to attack the jets when they were in the crucial take-off and landing phases. This proved successful on a number of occasions. While Mustangs could not overhaul an Me262 in level flight, they were able to position for attack by 'cutting the corner' when the jet entered a turn. A few Me262s are known to have fallen to Mustang gunnery when a jet engine failed with subsequent loss of speed. Overall it is probable that more Me262s were shot down by Mustangs than Mustangs shot down by these jets.

Defence tactics employed against Me262s involved the standard 'break' — pulling up while entering a sharp

At the end of hostilities in Europe the RAF planned to form Mustang squadrons in India to operate against the Japanese. Those aircraft reaching the theatre were too late to see action. Mustang IV KM730, seen here being flown by Flg Off Ford near Nagpur in October 1945, is a late P-51D with 'Zero length' rocket mounts under the wings. P. Knowles

turn to meet the attack head-on. With speed and firepower advantages, the Me262 employed 'hit and run' to shoot down Allied fighters. Providing the attacker was seen in sufficient time, Mustangs could usually evade. There are a number of recorded incidences when Mustang flights managed to outwit a succession of attacks by two, three or four Me262s for several minutes. As with other fighter types, once surprise was lost the advantage of speed was largely negated.

The combination of high performance and exceptional endurance were fundamental in the Mustang's employment as an escort fighter for the daylight bomber operations of the USAAF in both the European and Pacific Theatres of War. Positioned above their charges they were in a good position to execute dive, open fire and recovery tactics against enemy aircraft launching an assault on the bombers. If the enemy attempted to evade by going down, the Mustang's diving ability usually quickly negated any lead the pursued might have. However, the dominance obtained by USAAF Mustangs on long range escorts was due to a number of factors, not least poor enemy strategy and tactics. Pilot experience also played a major part as the general standard of both German and Japanese pilot training deteriorated rapidly in the final 18 months of hostilities. In short, the P-51 was an extremely good fighter, handled in a very effective way.

4
Combat Sortie –
Ground Attack

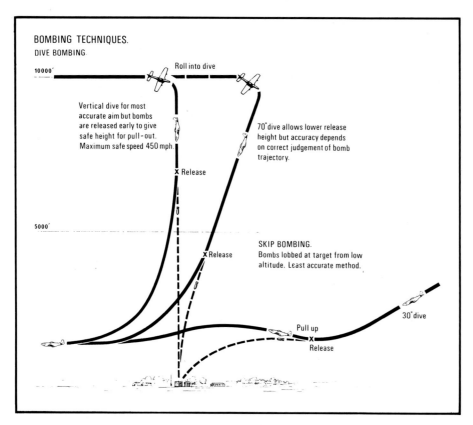

BOMBING TECHNIQUES.
DIVE BOMBING.

10000'

Roll into dive

Vertical dive for most accurate aim but bombs are released early to give safe height for pull-out. Maximum safe speed 450 mph.

70° dive allows lower release height but accuracy depends on correct judgement of bomb trajectory.

X Release

5000'

X Release

SKIP BOMBING.
Bombs lobbed at target from low altitude. Least accurate method.

30° dive

Pull up
X
Release

The original concept of a fighter was an aircraft armed and operated for the destruction of other aircraft in the air. In practice, the versatility of these fast, highly manoeuvrable warplanes enabled the military to employ them in a number of other roles. Most notable and successful was their use in attacks against an enemy's ground forces or war-aiding facilities, using standard armament or carried ordnance. The Mustang was employed extensively in ground attack roles by the USAAF, RAF and other Allied force operators during World War 2. However, the vulnerability of liquid-cooled engines to battle damage influenced USAAF policy whereby ground attack was primarily the task of the air-cooled, radial engined P-47 Thunderbolt. Nevertheless, P-51s of the US 8th, 9th and 15th Air Forces, frequently engaged in ground strafing actions in addition to their usual bomber escort duties. Attacks against airfields were often fruitful in regard to the destruction of enemy aircraft, but were also particularly dangerous as the small arms defences were usually formidable. Special pro-

cedures were evolved for strafing airfields with the aim of keeping losses to a minimum. Even so, during the course of hostilities, more P-51s were lost to ground fire, than to air combat.

By mid-April 1945, the imminent collapse of Nazi Germany and the fast-contracting battlefronts, brought large concentrations of aircraft on Luftwaffe bases in southern Germany and Czechoslovakia. Although it was known that the supply of aviation spirit in Germany was severely limited, Allied air leaders were concerned that these aircraft might be massing for some last-ditch strike against Allied forces. In consequence, 8th Air Force P-51 groups were despatched on several missions to seek out these large concentrations of enemy aircraft and destroy them by strafing. The following account of a P-51 operation on a strafing mission involves the same pilot featured in the escort mission of the opening chapter.

On a bright morning in April 1945, 1Lt George Vanden Heuvel finds he is

listed for an impending combat operation. At briefing it is revealed that the 361st Fighter Group will provide escort for a combat wing of B-24s attacking transportation targets northeast of Munich and thereafter to strafe enemy airfields in the area. Because of the distance involved — a round trip of some 1,300 miles — and the limitations on flight duration, two group forces will be despatched; one specifically assigned to escort and the other to strafing. The latter will fly the bomber escort route to the target but will then break away to attack airfields while the main escort force will continue with the bombers. Eight four-plane flights are scheduled for each force and Van finds he is to lead the third assigned to the strafing mission. Twenty of the P-51s will be from the 376th Fighter Squadron and the remainder from the 374th. Lt-Col Roy Caviness, the 361st Group commander, will lead the strafers. Being one of the longest missions undertaken by the group, flight time is calculated to be in the region of six hours. The trip will not, however, be as fatiguing as in past months for, with much of Western Europe now liberated, there is no requirement to climb to high altitude before Continental landfall.

Van's personal preparations follow his normal routine although some time is spent studying reports and maps relating to northwest Austria. This is an unfamiliar area to most of the pilots but fortunately there are some prominent rivers, notably the Inn, which can be used in locating objectives.

A few days earlier Van received a new Mustang which became the second *Mary Mine*. A P-51D-20-NA model, it incorporates minor changes that do not have major effect upon the operation and handling of the aircraft. The most significant is the substitution of metal-covered elevators in place of fabric, and a slightly decreased angle of incidence of the horizontal stabilisers. This provides better behaviour in high-speed dives, with less tail buffeting. On the other hand, it does change the stick forces with a requirement for greater physical effort to recover from a dive. The D-20-NA production batch also includes some changes to a few cockpit controls and introduces an electric priming fuel pump facility in addition to the hand pump. The vapour return line now runs to the fuselage tank and this is used from start. Another addition is tail warning radar, an AN/APS-13, intended to give the pilot warning of any aircraft approaching from the rear once it comes within the functional range of around a mile. This lightweight radar set is installed in the rear fuselage and the antenna — four small rods — projects from both sides of the tailfin. Once switched on, the radar works automatically, with warning given by both a red indicator light on the instrument panel and via an alarm bell. The new *Mary Mine* carries the squadron marking E9:Z.

Engine start is at 12.30hrs with the escort force being first off from Little Walden. The strafers commence take-off immediately afterwards and Van is airborne at precisely 12.45hrs. As he is flight leader, he goes into a gentle left-hand turn to allow the other element to position on his right and then tightens the initial orbit of the airfield in order to catch the two leading flights. Glowbright now takes a heading which will provide a direct line to the briefed rendezvous point with the bombers in the vicinity of Mannheim. Although the 361st escort force is on the same heading, it is already lost from sight.

The climb-out is gentle, with departure from the English coast at

13.09hrs. Height is gained steadily over France and an average speed of 250 IAS maintained by the close follow-my-leader formations. Once across the River Rhine, Glowbright calls for battle formation. The squadron is now spread over a two-mile front and at 14.25hrs the red-tailed B-24s they are to escort are seen near Speyer.

For an hour the strafing force flies with the B-24s, leaving them as they bomb a marshalling yard at Landshut at 15.30hrs. Now Glowbright gives radioed instructions to his force to close flights and split into two sections in trail. Glowbright then proceeds to reduce altitude to around 12,000ft, flying south until he picks up the airfield at Pocking. Columns of smoke rise from this Luftwaffe base, evidence that it has already been visited by strafers of some other group.

'This is Glowbright, don't think there is anything here for us. I'm going over to try the satellites.' The first of these landing grounds is at Reichersberg and fairly easily located between a river and a major highway. The procedure for strafing is well practised. First, the whole force over-flies its intended target at about 10,000ft and continues on the same course to the northeast for some miles. This ploy is to avoid alerting the enemy of the intended attack. Some 20 miles further on, Glowbright goes into a sweeping left-hand dive with four flights of the 376th Fighter

Squadron in trail. The remainder of the force also executes a 360° turn, but remains at the same altitude and will fly back across the target, acting as top cover to protect the strafers should any airborne enemy aircraft try to intercept.

White Flight now moves ahead of the rest; Glowbright is going to test the flak defences. If they appear substantial and dangerous he will radio for the following flights to abandon the attack. Yellow Flight moves under Red Flight in order to form a combined two-flight front. Having descended to about 500ft, both flights increase speed as they fly southwest, gradually dropping altitude as they go, but just keeping White Flight in sight above the treetops. Van reaches down and switches to a main fuel cell before jettisoning the two 108gal drop tanks. As the eight Mustangs descend still closer to the ground, Van twists in 3° of elevator tab to trim *Mary Mine* slightly nose-up. This is a safety precaution so that if his attention is momentarily distracted the P-51 will climb rather than mush into the forests they are hurtling over — now at little more than 100ft.

Van hopes that Glowbright is on the correct heading. It is easy to become disorientated at this height and speed.

Below:
Van's sketch map of the attack on Reichersberg landing ground.

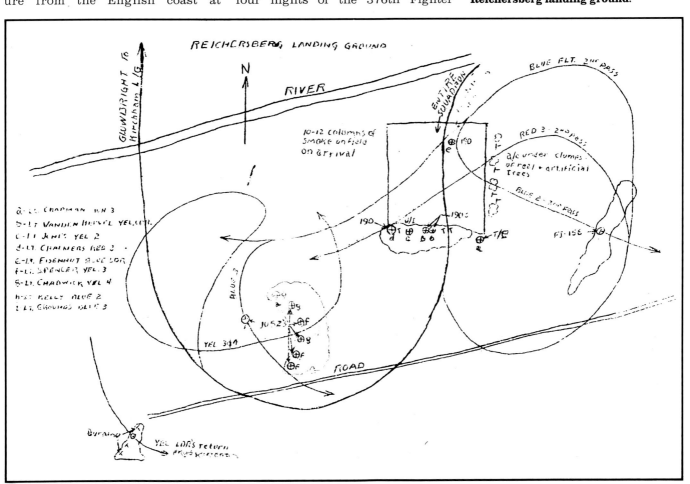

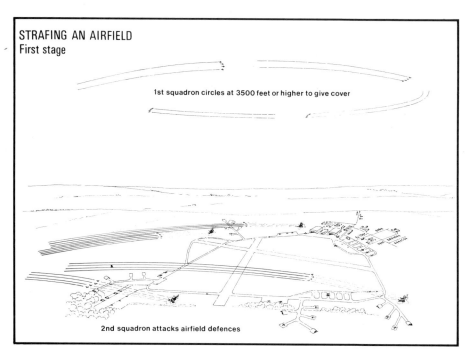

STRAFING AN AIRFIELD
First stage

1st squadron circles at 3500 feet or higher to give cover

2nd squadron attacks airfield defences

The landing ground was lost from view when the squadron dived down and Van does not know what landmarks the colonel had picked out to ensure a true run. The terrain now opens out into rolling wooded country. Van estimates the objective, an area of woods and fields beside a broad road in a shallow valley, should appear at any moment; he presses on the stick to take *Mary Mine* down until the aircraft is literally skimming the treetops. Ahead he can see foliage swaying from the slipstream of White Flight. This hedge-hopping approach is essential to gain that element of surprise before any anti-aircraft defences are alerted and can open up on the Mustangs. The next second the river appears and the ground-hugging Mustangs are over and past. Off to the left, Van sees partly camouflaged aircraft parked around the edge of a wood. Quick application of rudder skids the Mustang so that he can get the enemy aircraft in his sight and at 800yd he opens fire, seeing the bullets churn up dust as they strike the ground short of the target. Instant manoeuvring of *Mary Mine* brings the bullet pattern up into the enemy aircraft. At 300yd his target explodes in flames and another to which Van now directs his fire also ignites a moment before *Mary Mine* wings over the treetops. Once past this small piece of woodland, Van brings his Mustang down to less than 20ft from the ground and dodges behind another wood. Out of the corner of his eye he has seen the flash of tracers from some alert German gunner. A glance right confirms that Yellow 2, his wingman Don Jones, is still in position. Yellow

Below:
A Mustang pilot 'walks' his fire into a line of parked aircraft. USAF

Flight does not begin to climb for altitude until three or four miles from the airfield. White Flight is turning south. Glowbright is going to have a look at the other Pocking satellite across the river at Kircham. The flights climb to around 8,000ft, high enough to be clear of any small arms fire that the enemy may discharge at them. There is no sign of the other element of Yellow Flight but Blue Flight, coming up behind, appears to be intact.

Van considers that Glowbright is veering too far to the east: 'Yorkshire Yellow Leader to Glowbright: we just passed the castle near the river, the target should be coming up to the west any second now.'

'Okay Van, I got it'. Glowbright turns west, moving across Red and Yellow Flights. Van increases power to bring *Mary Mine* and Yellow Flight up on the opposite side of the leader's flight. The instruments indicate he is making just under 360 IAS. They are in a shallow dive from 8,000ft while crossing their objective. Again Glowbright continues on for some miles, executes a 360° turn and takes the squadron down to 'the deck'. They are on a southwest heading over well wooded countryside. Glowbright and his wingman have pulled ahead to test the flak defences. There is no call to abandon the pass — but where is the landing ground? Van jinks the nose down but can see nothing but clumps of trees and meadows. Just as he feels that he has missed the location, he sees something in the woodland scrub to his left. Left rudder skids *Mary Mine* round. A quick visual check over his left shoulder to make sure this action has not brought him into Yellow 2's line of fire. It would not be the first time that an element leader had committed the folly of getting himself shot down by his wingman. Jones is well clear so Van quickly returns his attention to the object in the trees which can now be seen to be an aircraft, although too well camouflaged with foliage for the type to be identified. Van hits the gun trigger at about 500yd range and immediately there is a slight kick as six 0.50s unleash 80 rounds a second. The next moment Van is pulling back on the stick to clear some pines. As he wings over his burning target he recognises it as a twin-engined Me410. There is some small arms fire from the ground and once more Van pulls *Mary Mine* down to 'cut the daisies' until well out of range. At two miles from the airfield he recovers to altitude and finds his faithful wingman is still with him.

Glowbright and White Flight are no longer to be seen so Van decides to return to Reichersberg where there appeared to be more targets and less flak. Locating the river, he descends to skip across fields and woods, finally

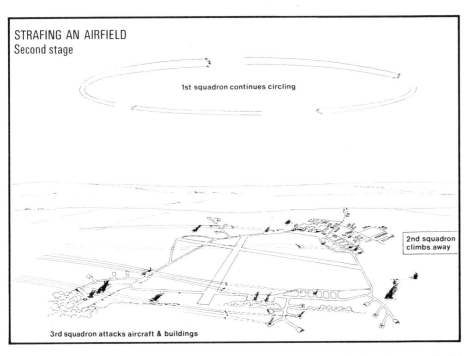

STRAFING AN AIRFIELD
Second stage

1st squadron continues circling

2nd squadron climbs away

3rd squadron attacks aircraft & buildings

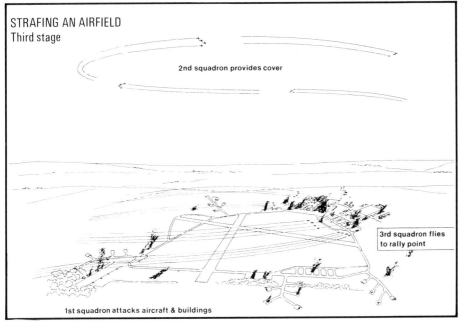

STRAFING AN AIRFIELD
Third stage

2nd squadron provides cover

3rd squadron flies to rally point

1st squadron attacks aircraft & buildings

spotting a Ju52 transport partly concealed beside another wood. Skidding *Mary Mine* to line up his gunsight, fire is immediately opened, walking the bullets into his target as before. Just as Van is about to stop firing, orange tracers leave his guns, a sign that ammunition is almost exhausted. It is policy to include a number of tracer bullets before the last 30 rounds to warn a pilot of depleted ammunition. The transport he has just shot up shows no sign of catching fire as Van hurtles away across the countryside. Some three miles on he starts to climb, checking all instruments for any warning signs that the engine or some vital component may have been hit by ground fire. Yellow 2 is still flying a few hundred feet away from *Mary Mine's* left wingtip.

The squadron has arranged to rendezvous over a distinctive bend in the River Inn. As *Mary Mine* climbs, Glowbright is heard calling over the VHF radio: 'Yorkshire Squadron make it to rendezvous in the next two minutes. Then we'll head home.'

Presently four or five other Mustangs are seen orbiting at 8,000ft. The yellow noses and tails identify them as 376th aircraft. Yellow 3 and 4 are found and the flight reassembles for the journey home. Five aircraft are missing from the squadron.

'Red 3 to Glowbright. Red 4 went down at Kircham. He blew.'

'Okay', responds Glowbright. There is nothing else to say. Red 4 has probably paid the supreme price, but everyone hopes he survived.

The formation spreads out for the long flight home. The Mustang is easy to fly when properly trimmed out and most men relax with a cigarette. The gauges on *Mary Mine* show sufficient fuel to reach Little Walden, now some 610 miles away.

Mary Mine's wheels touch down at home base at 18.45hrs. Van has been

Below:
Well-placed bursts of 'fifty calibre' explode an aircraft's fuel tanks.
Via D. Morris

Right:
A Dornier takes fire from a hail of 'Point Fifties'. Via D. Morris

in the air exactly six hours. The group has had a successful day with a total of 17 enemy aircraft credited as destroyed on the ground and five damaged. Van has obtained three destroyed and one damaged credits for the expenditure of 1,575 rounds of ammunition. Several of the Mustangs have battle damage and two have failed to return, although it is hoped one has landed at an Allied base in France. On this day 8th Air Force Mustangs have shot up over 700 Luftwaffe aircraft on airfields and landing grounds in southeast Germany. The cost is 31 of their own number missing in action.

Right:
Squadron combat report of strafing claims.

~~CONFIDENTIAL~~

COMBAT REPORT

Confidential as claims Report No 7 30 May 1945.

A. Strafing
B. 16 April 1945 F.O. 1997A 8AF
C. 376th Fighter Squadron
D. 1550
E. Reichersberg, Germany
F. 5 mi visibility
G. Ju 52's, FW's, Storch and U/I's
H. 2 FW 190's destroyed - 1st Lt. George R. Vanden Heuvel, 0-377674
   1 Ju 52 damaged - 1st Lt. George R. Vanden Heuvel, 0-377674
   1 FW 190 destroyed - 1st Lt. Van C. Eisenhut, 0-805955
   3 Ju 52's destroyed - 1st Lt. Herbert G. Spencer, 0-2000421
   3 Ju 52's destroyed - 1st Lt. Lewis P. Chadwick, 0-720785
   1 FW 190 destroyed - 1st Lt. Allen J. Chalmers, 0-720786
   1 T/E U/I destroyed - 1st Lt. Harry M. Chapman, 0-720786
   1 Ju 52 damaged - 2nd Lt. Duane Grounds, 0-720841
   1 U/I destroyed - 2nd Lt. Donald W. Jones, 0-721421
   1 Storch destroyed - 2nd Lt. Marion C. Kelly, 0-720721

I. At 1550 GLOWBRIGHT, Lt. Col. Caviness, made a pass at Reichersberg landing ground followed by the rest of Yorkshire Squadron. The pass was made NE to SW, with a small left turn off the field, breaking into a right turn to go over and investigate Kircham landing ground. White 3, Lt. Chapman, fired on a twin engine airplane in the open at the south corner of the field which caught fire and burned. This was the only undamaged aircraft in the open, all others were already burning, or under the trees. (See sketch). Yellow leader, Lt. Vanden Heuvel, began firing at 800 yards to the SW. As he got in range he saw there were two a/c parked together. One blew up at 300 yards and the other began to burn as Yellow leader pulled up over them, and identified them as FW 190's. Yellow 2, Lt. Jones, began firing into the same woods until he saw the sun glint on an a/c parked behind the trees. He fired at it until it exploded. Yellow 3 and Yellow 4 did not fire, but as they pulled up they saw several a/c in the woods SW of the field and went back for them. Red 3 leading the right edge of the flight), Lt. Chalmers, saw an FW 190 at the right edge of the woods at the SW edge too late to fire so he made a circle to the left and made a west to east pass across the field, pulling his strikes up into the cockpit and seeing the airplane burn as he passed over it. Blue flight did not fire on this pass, but turned around to the left for another NE - SW pass. This time, Blue leader, Lt. Eisenhut, found an FW 190 on the north edge of the field and fired from 400 yards until the a/c burned as he passed over it. Blue 2, Lt. Kelly, fired at a Fiesler Storch, but it wouldn't burn. Blue 3, Lt. Grounds, shot up a Ju 52 which also wouldn't burn. Meanwhile, Yellow 3 and Yellow 4, Lt. Spencer and Lt. Chadwick, set up a gunnery pattern of their own on several Ju 52's parked along the west edge of the patch of the woods about 500 yards SW of the field, making passes from west to east. In about five passes they each caused three Ju 52's to burn up (a total of six). After his pass on Kircham a/f yellow leader, Lt. Vanden Heuvel, came back and made a pass at another Ju 52 in this same woods, but, though it was clobbered, the a/c refused to burn.

J. 1st Lt. George R. Vanden Heuvel, Yellow leader, E9V P51D10 44-64005 *1575 rds. expended
   1st Lt. Van C. Eisenhut, Blue leader, E9L P51D15 44-15752 *900 rds expended
   1st Lt. Herbert G. Spencer, Yellow three, E9U P51D10 44-14806
   1st Lt. Lewis P. Chadwick, Yellow four, E9H P51D15 44-11369 1600 rds expended
   1st Lt. Allen J. Chalmers, Red three, E9L P51D15 44-15752 600 rds expended
   1st Lt. Harry M. Chapman, White Three, E9X P51D5 44-13391 *600 rds expended
   1st Lt. Duane Grounds, Blue three, E9G P51D10 44-14251 300 rds expended
   2nd Lt. Donald W. Jones, Yellow two, E9L P51D10 44-14685 800 rds expended
   2nd Lt. Marion C. Kelly, Blue two, E9C P51D15 44-15040 336 rds expended

*denotes total rds expended for entire mission.

GEORGE R. VANDEN HEUVEL,
1st Lt., Air Corps,
0-377674

42

Above:
The elements close up for the long flight home.   Via D. Morris

Left:
The flight 'peels off' preparatory to making landing approaches.
M. Olmsted

Below:
A squadron returns to its home field from the long haul.   Via D. Morris

Arms for Ground Attack

Right:
To increase the Mustang's firepower when ground strafing, in the summer of 1944 the USAAF in the UK developed auxiliary gun pods which could be carried on the standard underwing shackles. Each pod held two 0.50in calibre machine guns with 340 rounds per gun, enclosed in a sheet steel casing and weighing 450lb in total. If required the gun pod could be jettisoned in flight. A pod with a single gun was also developed but neither weapon was taken beyond the experimental stage.
USAAF

Below:
Attaching a 500lb General Purpose (GP) bomb to wing shackles was a difficult task without proper jacking equipment. In many squadrons — this is 334th — an extension cradle was improvised from steel scrap and wood to enable bombs to be elevated by a standard hydraulic trolley-jack. Even then it remained a difficult task and also required a crowbar to line up the two sling hooks with the shackles.
L. Nitschke

Above:
Two 500lb M43 GP bombs on a 355th Fighter Squadron P51-B. Two 1,000lb bombs could be carried but their use was discontinued by most operational units because of the adverse effect on the aircraft's handling and performance, in addition to over-stressing the wings.

Below:
Air-to-ground rocket projectiles were used by RAF Mustang squadrons in Italy. The British-manufactured guide rails held four missiles with 60lb warheads under each wing. However, the drag of a full load took over 100mph off the Mustang's combat speed at low altitudes. IWM

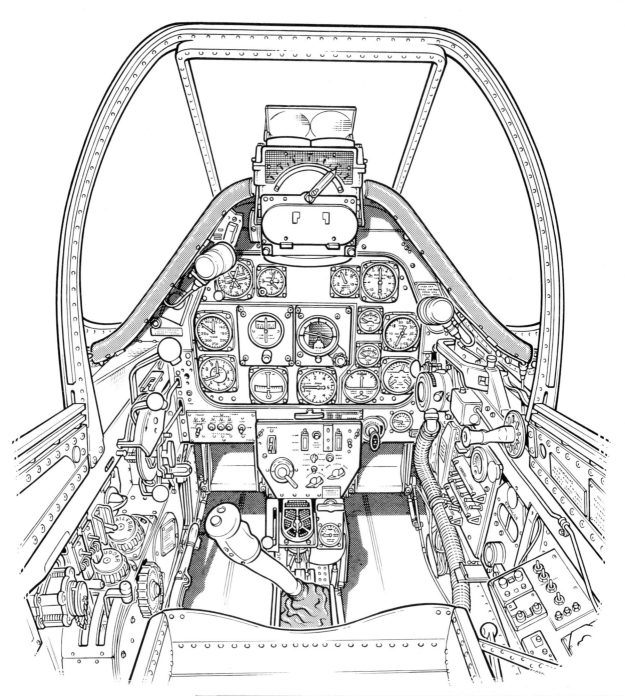

Above:
P51-D cockpit layout.
Drawing by Mike Keep

Right:
1 Flare Pistol Opening, **2** Coolant
Radiator Air Control Switch, **3** Oil
Radiator Air Control Switch, **4** Landing
Light Switch, **5** Fluorescent Light
Switch, **6** Flap Control Handle,
7 Carburettor Air Controls, **8** Rudder
Trim Tab Control, **9** Aileron Trim Tab
Control, **10** Elevator Trim Tab Control,
11 Landing Gear Control, **12** Throttle.
Via D. Morris

5
Individual Opinion

While laudatory views of Mustangs predominate, differing emphasis on virtues and vices encountered are undoubtedly influenced by experiences of particular pilots. The following personal statements reflect this, but at the same time highlight aspects of Mustang operation that would be endorsed by most men who flew it in combat.

Robert H. Riemensnider, a commander of the 55th Fighter Squadron, with considerable experience of flying P-51Ds in Europe states:

'Basically the enemy was faced with similar problems in his single-engined fighters to those which we had in ours. We may have been advised of the various performance advantages and disadvantages they had in comparison with our aircraft, but in practice these were generally insufficient to be critical. Operational factors — the type of mission undertaken, an aircraft's loading, the altitude flown and so on — had far more influence on whether or not we were at an advantage when enemy fighters were encountered. Our regular disadvantage, particularly in the early stages of a mission, was that we were carrying fuel for four to six hours' duration, whereas the Me109s and FW190s usually expected to be airborne for not much more than an hour. In other words, we were carrying a great deal of extra weight that was going to affect performance and manoeuvrability until it was partly burned up. If we got into a fight soon after penetration of enemy airspace and had to get rid of our drop tanks,

Below:
Maj Robert H. Riemensnider.
R. Riemensnider

the main tanks would still be near to full. The lighter your aircraft the better its performance and manoeuvrability in a dogfight — but we didn't look for dogfights and neither did the enemy.

'Air fighting was usually a case of chase, shoot and recover, whatever type you were flying. Very little air-to-air firing in fighter-fighter combat was played other than straight behind the intended victim or at an angled pass. To hit the other fellow while you were pulling Gs in a turn was generally a matter of luck. Centrifugal pull took the bullets as soon as they left the gun barrels and their trajectory was way behind the point of aim in your gunsight. You could allow over-lead in your sighting in an effort to compensate for this fudge factor, but whether or not you scored hits was still down to luck. The K-14 gyroscopic gunsight was a big improvement and a great aid to deflection shooting. It did compensate to a great degree with G-forces if firing while pulling a turn. It was very sensitive and required very smooth co-ordination of stick and rudder; even mild application of control pressure caused the aiming dot to dance all over the display. I had previously flown the twin-engined P-38 Lightning where the nose-mounted armament made for an ideal gun platform. Ranging wasn't the problem it was with the P-51 and other fighters which had wing-mounted armament where the fire converged. In our outfit the guns were adjusted for a point of convergence 300yd ahead where, theoretically, they gave an approximately 8×10ft bullet pattern. In practice, because of the speed of closure, it was not easy to achieve that exact range when you hit the gun trigger. So there was a tendency for pilots to open fire at a target further off and hold a long burst as they closed. If you got in a correctly ranged burst, it was highly destructive. In my opinion the six 0.50in calibre guns of the P-51D were adequate for the job we were doing.

'I preferred the P-38 for ground strafing. As said, it was a better gun platform, but having two engines was an important factor in that we felt there was more chance of coming home. I am told that statistics don't bear this out and that the Mustang with the Merlin was more reliable than the Lightning with two Allisons. The

most troublesome thing with the Merlin was plug fouling, for long flights at cruise settings to conserve fuel caused excessive carbonising. Often all plugs had to be changed after a mission. Another engine problem that came with using extra high octane fuel and the high temperatures it created was valve stem stretching. Every so often the groundcrew had to reset the valve clearances. There was a limit to how many times this could be done and eventually the engine had to be overhauled and new valves installed.

'The Mustang was an easy plane to pilot, light on the controls and responsive. In common with all single-engined aircraft it would spin out if too tight a turn was pulled, but it could turn as tight as most other types before this happened. If you did pull the turn in too much you would soon experience a half-snap, and if still held you were into a spin. Left-hand spins were more violent than right-hand spins where engine torque added to the oscillations. If the throttle wasn't cut immediately the aircraft could enter a power-on spin which was highly dangerous — for you and the aircraft. In comparison, the P-38 would shudder if the turn was pulled too tight before a stall. You had little warning in a P-51; the first you knew was a half-snap into the turn. There was no real problem in recovering from a spin; but it just wasn't the thing you wanted to happen in combat.

'The Mustang was fast and had good acceleration in a dive; it was easy to get into excessive dive speeds. The aircraft gave you warning as it would start to porpoise and there was normally no difficulty in recovering. The same couldn't be said of the P-38 which was red-lined at certain speeds. If these were exceeded in a dive you took your life in your hands with a high chance of the aircraft breaking up or boring a hole in the ground with you still in it.

'I rated the P-51 cockpit high on comfort. There were never any temperature control problems at high altitude, and the heating system was good. Perhaps my opinion was influenced by having been chilled time and again in P-38s — you could freeze to death in that cockpit in winter. The Mustang's seat comfort was another matter, although the long duration of our missions was the real problem. We

sat on the dinghy pack and the inflation bottle always seemed to be in the wrong place, making your tailbone ache.

'Like all single propeller fighters with a powerful engine up front, directional stability had to be watched. However, it was less affected by torque than the Curtiss P-40 which had far less power. Any increase or decrease in air speed or power setting with the Mustang meant changes in rudder pressure to maintain your course. To fly "feet off" it was necessary to readjust the rudder trim tab following every power or airspeed change otherwise the plane entered a skid. Engine torque was particularly noticeable on take-off when you were drawing full power before picking up flying speed. We automatically turned in 5° of right rudder trim before starting the run, even so you had to push real hard on the right rudder pedal to counteract the torque and keep her straight while the airpeed built up. As the speed increased the air velocity over the rudder, you could relax the pressure. As I've said, this technique was common to all single-engined fighters, but because of the power available and the heavy loads usually carried, take-off demanded special vigilance in a Mustang, as did the climb to altitude.

'With a full fuselage tank the centre of gravity was moved back, making the P-51 unstable for anything but level flight. Until the bulk of the

48

fuselage tank was used up it was just about impossible to trim the aircraft for hands-off, so it was standard operating procedure to use that fuel first. Turns had to be gentle for a full fuselage tank produced a reverse effect on the controls if you pulled too tight. In a turn you naturally held the stick back. You would then find that without further movement of the stick the aircraft would start to quickly tighten the turn. To prevent this, forward pressure on the stick was required. Once the gas in the fuselage tank was depleted to about 35gal, then normal control returned. Anyone who tried tight manoeuvres while it was still full was soon going to get into big trouble.

'The more flight time I had in the P-51, the more confident I became in its suitability for the missions we had to fly. It had speed, range, and an all-round versatility that was unsurpassed by any of its contemporaries in combat service. Another advantage, though not from a pilot's point of view, was the economy. It cost much less to produce and was considerably more economical on fuel consumption than its counterparts, the P-38 and P-47.'

Curtis Smart, a pilot in the 385th Fighter Squadron, 364th Fighter Group, recalls other aspects of flying the P-51 over Europe:

Above:
Bob Riemensnider's personal P-51D, 44-13905, coded KI:Y. R. Riemensnider

'The Mustang was a pilot's airplane, you didn't get into it, you put it on like your parachute. That statement may have been made about other fighters; all I know is that it was true of the P-51. It was such an easy airplane to fly, light on the controls and without any real vices. Once you had learned to fly it, you had to work at getting into trouble during normal flight.

'Prior to my arrival, our outfit had flown P-38s and the surviving pilots were always telling newcomers like myself about the benefits of having two engines. I never flew the P-38, I was trained from the beginning in single-engined fighters. Those who flew the P-38s loved them and even today when the group gets together, you will have heated arguments on the merits of the two planes. The P-51 had no problems with compressibility in a dive; we had longer legs — that is, we were able to escort the bombers on longer missions; our kills increased and I believe we lost fewer planes. The worries of the ex-P-38 people were centred on the vast distances we had to fly with just a single engine. Many of the P-38 guys could tell you a personal story of coming home on one engine. The Rolls-Royce Packard engine in the P-51 proved to be extraordinarily reliable. Externally, the engine didn't look too attractive, it was roughcast and didn't have the finish of the English version. But inside the engine, where it counted, it was built to the design specifications and tolerances. Its output and ruggedness were remarkable, it took a lot of abuse at our hands and as long as you didn't get a hole in the coolant system, it would get you home. There was a minor problem with plug fouling due to low power settings we used for long missions. Rough running was avoided by periodically advancing the power for a few seconds.

'There was always a need for extra speed, particularly when in contact with the German jets which had near a 100mph advantage. In our squadron someone decided that the maximum manifold pressure we could pull was too conservative and had their crew chief set the engine controls so that we could draw several inches more. Most of us followed suit until the North American Technical Representative arrived at Honington and discovered what we were doing. He nearly had a fit: he said we were going to blow the engines up if we continued to draw these high manifold pressures. So we had to put them back although I don't recall any adverse effects from these high settings. Another effort made to get more speed was to use shoe polish on the leading edge of the wings and tail and buff them. The idea being to reduce drag. I guess it made very little difference.

'Many pilots had their crew chiefs make small modifications to their personal aircraft. I found difficulty in seeing the fuel gauges which were in a well on the floor of the cockpit next to my feet. So I had my crew chief fix up some lights to illuminate them. On the first mission flown with these new lights, they worked fine, but I found out too late that they had been installed in such a way as to obstruct the relief tube so I couldn't pull it up. I had a real problem!

'With the built-in fuel tanks and extra drop tanks the P-51 could range further than any other single-engined fighter of its day. It is my belief that some missions were as long as eight hours or more. Seven hours was my longest mission and was flown on 17 April 1945. The airplane designers never had flights of such long duration in mind; the P-51 was adapted to meet an operational requirement for extra-long range. The airplane proved up to the task but other problems arose. There was pilot fatigue: sitting in that small cockpit on a CO_2 bottle in the dinghy, and with the sun beating down on the Plexiglas for hour after hour it was difficult to stay alert, and tired pilots make mistakes. A major concern was navigation. In later years the development of radio and electronic aids made navigation child's play. During World War 2 navigation for fighters was by dead reckoning or pilotage (that is by visual landmarks) with help from radio direction finders. Frequently we had to fly through weather extending from the deck up to 20,000ft or more. Navigation under these conditions was, to say the least, difficult. The problem really started when you became separated from the rest of your flight after a dogfight that may have covered a radius of many miles and you found yourself alone above an undercast 200 or 300 miles from home. Your only lifeline was the radio with which you could, hopefully, call the direction finder station for a bearing to fly. The radio saved hundreds of lost souls but it was a very tenuous lifeline.

'There was another angle to long range missions at high altitude that should not be overlooked: oxygen supply. When the P-51 was developed for extra-long range the oxygen supply was increased. The low pressure demand system used in the P-51 automatically supplied the right amount of oxygen at any altitude for the pilot. But if needed, you had controls to bypass the automatic system and obtain 100% pure oxygen continuously. If you did, consumption rate doubled; I learned the hard way just how vital oxygen was to our job. On my second mission, the group did an escort to Berlin. This was an exciting proposition for a new, green replacement pilot. We got into a dogfight with the Germans that carried my flight leader and myself from around 28,000ft to the deck and back. On level-off at altitude I had time to run a check around the cockpit. To my chagrin, I discovered I was about out of oxygen. To this day I don't know if the system developed a leak or in the excitement of my first dogfight I literally consumed my oxygen. I informed the Squadron Operation Officer, for whom I was flying wingman, and told him the problem. We dropped down on the deck and, to avoid flak, hedge-hopped out of Germany. While this protected us from the heavy and medium flak, it put us in the range of mobile, deadly light flak. We were fortunate to avoid these flak positions. Everything was going fine until we got to Holland. We flew right over a V-weapon launching site and all hell broke loose when the Germans opened up with everything they had. I had heard of the orange golf balls and now I was seeing them for the first time as they curved around behind my wing to impact against my tail. We made it to an emergency base at St Trond in Belgium but my Mustang was so damaged it was later junked.

'As a sidelight to this incident, this P-51 had previously been used by a pilot who finished his tour of duty and the aircraft had been reassigned to me. Its nickname was *Damn Yankee* and as a Southerner I couldn't go with that and told my crew chief to remove the name when I returned from the mission. The Germans saved him the job. I had two more P-51s after that. I named them *Estrellita II* and *III*.

'The big worry for me with the Mustang was the possibility of taking a hit in the coolant system while strafing. If that happened you didn't have a lot of time to get out before the engine was on fire — you were too busy at low altitude to catch the gauges and see what was happening. The first thing most pilots knew was the engine starting to burn and then it was too late. Luckily it never happened to me.'

———————

The Merlin Mustang had good standing with the Royal Air Force who employed the type in a number of combat roles. The largest force was deployed to escort RAF Bomber Command heavy bombers on daylight operations. William Fleming was one of the Mustang pilots engaged in these sorties:

'When I joined No 154 Squadron at Biggin Hill in 1944, it was equipped with Spitfire VIIs with pressurised cockpits for high altitude flying. As part of London defences our main duties were to attempt to intercept the very high-flying Ju86 reconnaissance aircraft which were "spotting" in connection with the V-1 and V-2 attacks on London and the South-East. As the V-bomb attacks reduced, the squadron started bomber escort operations, but we were limited by the short range of our Spitfires. It was decided, therefore, to rearm the squadron with Mustang IVs which were received brand-new. Prior to the aircraft being delivered we received copies of the Pilots' Notes to read. After the very official Air Ministry handbooks for other planes we had flown, we were rather surprised by the racy terms in which the Mustang notes were couched, although they

Below:
Flt Lt William Fleming.

gave us all the information we needed. The Spitfire was an aircraft with few, if any, vices and one had to be very ham-handed to get into serious trouble. We were appalled, therefore, to read about some of the Mustang's "nasty habits", chief of which was instability and reversibility of controls which occurred on violent manoeuvring or landing with a full fuselage tank when the centre of gravity of the plane was upset. We therefore viewed the arrival of the Mustangs with some apprehension.

'One day when some of us who were not flying and were sitting in the dispersal hut, one of the ground staff came in to announce that the first Mustang was on the circuit. We dashed outside and climbed on to the top of an air raid shelter to watch the silver Mustang land, fearing that all kinds of terrible things would happen to it. It made a perfect approach and three-point landing, taxied up to the Flying Control Tower and out stepped a small, blonde, very attractive ATA girl! We slunk back into the hut with our tails between our legs. With the arrival of more Mustangs we began to familiarise ourselves with the aircraft, and in particular with the cockpits. The wingspan and length was very similar to the Spitfire, but it looked a much bigger and more substantial aircraft and was, of course, heavier. The Packard-built Merlin V-1650 was very similar to the Merlins in our Spitfires and we found them to be very

reliable in use. I was informed, however, by our Engineering Officer (EO), that although very well built the degree of precision was not as great as in Rolls-Royce-built engines. In British-built engines a part transferred from one engine to another would always fit, but this was not always so in the Packard Merlins. Our EO may, of course, have been biased.

'The aircraft looked silver in colour, being uncamouflaged, with top of the engine cowling painted matt green to prevent glare from the sun. The pilots used to polish the fuselages periodically to induce a few extra mph.

'Sitting in the cockpit, the first thing which struck one was its spaciousness compared with a Spitfire or Hurricane. With its bubble canopy, visibility all round was first class, much better than in other aircraft I had flown. The Mustang IIIs, with their Malcolm hoods, were not so good; particularly when fitted with the larger gyro gunsights. There were many differences in the cockpit layout compared with Spitfires and Hurricanes. The thing I missed at first was the standard blind-flying panel common to British-built aircraft, which was always in the same position on the instrument panel. In the Mustang, the same blind-flying instruments were present, but in a different layout which took a little time to get used to. The undercarriage lever was on the left-hand side, which obviated the necessity of changing

hands on the control column on take-off as one had to do in the Spitfire where the lever was on the right. The brakes were operated by pressing the rudder controls, whereas in the Spitfire and Hurricane they were operated by a lever on the control column in conjunction with the rudder pedals. The boost gauge was calibrated in inches of mercury as opposed to pounds per square inch in the Spitfires and Hurricanes. The radio transmit button was situated on the throttle quadrant, whereas in the Spitfire and Hurricane it was on the radio channel control box. This latter difference nearly caused a disaster when later I was flying Spitfires again. During a practice dive-bombing sortie at Selsey, I forgetfully pressed the button on the throttle to transmit, and to my horror then realised this was the bomb release button. On looking down I saw a small fishing boat which had just been missed by the stray bomb!

Below:
No 309 (Polish) Squadron received Mustang IIIs in December 1944. At this date few of the USAAF equivalent, the P-51B and C, were still being used on combat missions from the UK. The Mk III, however, remained the most numerous RAF Mustang to the end of hostilities. All UK-based Mustang IIIs in operational squadrons were fitted with the Malcolm hood by the end of 1944 but few fin extensions were to be seen until the following spring.
Sekcja Film-Foto

'Having familiarised ourselves with the cockpit layout, we started doing our first flights. Starting-up was similar to the Spitfire and Hurricane. There was, however, a danger if the engine was over-primed that flames from the exhaust would spread over the engine cowling; this did happen occasionally.

'Taxying was easy once one had got used to the operation of the brakes. Visibility was fairly good, the nose was not so bulbous as on the Spitfire — more like a Hurricane. The undercarriage was wider than the Spitfire and the tailwheel was steerable over 6° on either side with the control column held back beyond the neutral position. With the radiator being situated under the fuselage, similar to the Hurricane, there was little or no danger of overheating on the ground as there was in the case of the Spitfire where the radiators, being under the wings, did not get the benefit of propeller slipstream. On take-off it was recommended that the tailwheel be kept down as long as possible to take advantage of the steerable wheel. This helped to control the rather strong swing due to propeller torque. Usually we took-off with 15° flap down — this was essential when carrying a full fuel load. The flap was raised on reaching a safe height and airspeed.

'As part of the pre-take-off check a bar under the flap lever was moved across to limit the flaps to 15°. We called this the "combat bar" as it was left in position until coming into land so that 15° flap could be lowered quickly to allow for the Mustang to turn more tightly. On one occasion my Number 2 forgot to move the bar when coming in to land behind me. Unable to reduce his speed, he hit the runway and bounced over me, bursting a tyre in the process but fortunately swinging off the runway away from me. I was not too pleased!

'There were two teething troubles we encountered when first operating Mustangs. Firstly, on take-off, sometimes when raising the undercarriage one of the wheel struts would foul the fairings which dropped to allow the wheels to be retracted. This in turn ruptured a small piston in the system and prevented the undercarriage from being lowered hydraulically. To lower the wheels in these circumstances necessitated pulling the red emergency knob to allow them to drop down under their own weight and rock the plane to try to lock the undercarriage. This only happened to me once. Fortunately the wheels did lock down although the indicator lights showed that they were still up. The other problem concerned the wing drop tanks. These were impregnated papier-mâché with capacity for 100gal of fuel. To begin with there was a problem in fitting them and it was not uncommon for one of the tanks to drop off on take-off. As we took-off in pairs with perhaps only 50-75yd between each pair on the runway, it was an unnerving sight to see a tank bouncing back towards you, spewing petrol all over the runway! Fortunately, no serious accident happened, but the aircraft which had lost one of its tanks had to return to base.

'Returning to my first flight, I achieved a fairly good take-off, bearing in mind the instructions in the handbook, and spent a pleasant hour familiarising myself with the flying characteristics of the Mustang. It was a very nice plane to fly. The controls were very light and positive, particularly when compared with the Spitfire VII which, because of the pressurised cockpit, had all control systems enter the cockpit through sealed conduits. The rate of roll was quicker than the Spitfire, also a much faster initial rate of dive. The Spitfire, being a lighter aircraft, could outclimb the Mustang — initially, anyway — and could easily out-turn it. Even with 15° flap down a Mustang could not stay with a Spitfire, which could do steep climbing turns on full power at speeds as low as 90-100mph.

'Providing that the fuselage tank was no more than half full, aerobatics were a delight to perform. Only once did I try to perform aerobatics with a

Below:
Flg Off Ron Palmer piloting a No 154 Squadron Mustang IVA over Kent in February 1945. No 154 was one of the first squadrons to receive this British version of the P-51K. P. Knowles

full tank (unknown to me) and I just fell out of the sky from rolls, loops and rolls off the top until I realised what was happening. Landing on the first occasion nearly ended in disaster. The approach speed on the circuit turning in was 150mph "over the hedge" at 120mph and touchdown at about 100mph — faster than a Spitfire or a Hurricane. Unfortunately, I misjudged the height of the aircraft, bounced, stalled and dropped a wing sharply, corrected this with opposite rudder and proceeded down the runway like a kangaroo. Fortunately, nothing broke. Once mastered, however, I found the Mustang to be a much easier plane to land, more so than the Spitfire which, because of the relatively low wing loading and narrow undercarriage, tended to be rather "skittish" and would lift a wing, particularly when landing in a cross-wind. The Mustang just sat down and stayed down!

'As two of the runways at Biggin Hill were too short for safety with a fully-laden Mustang, the squadron moved to Hunsdon near Ware in Hertfordshire at the beginning of March 1945 to form a Wing with

Above:

The RAF did not receive Mustangs with the all-round vision 'bubble' canopy until some five months after the USAAF had introduced the type into service. Most British deliveries came from the Dallas, Texas plant as Mustang IVAs — the P-51K. The only major difference between the 'D' and 'K' models was the latter's Aeroproducts propeller which was lighter and had a faster pitch change than the Hamilton on the 'D'. However, the Aeroproducts was considered more troublesome, with blade imbalance problems that caused vibration. S. Clay

No 611 Squadron, also flying Mustang IVs. There we stayed until the beginning of April when No 154 Squadron was disbanded and our aircraft handed over to a Canadian squadron, much to our disgust. Apparently it was a political move to allow the Canadians to have a squadron of Mustangs to escort their own heavy bomber squadrons. The No 154 Squadron pilots were dispersed and some of my colleagues and I were

posted to No 126 Squadron at Bentwaters, flying Mustang IIIs and later IVs.

'In all I took part in 20 long range escort missions with Nos 154 and 126 Squadrons. The duration of these trips varied from three to more than five hours. Our operating height was usually 20,000-25,000ft but on one occasion, because of bad weather, we had to climb to over 35,000ft when the handling of the aircraft became very sloppy. The number of bombers escorted ranged from 1,000 to as few as 20 in a specialist operation.

'RAF heavy bombers, being more used to flying at night, did not operate in tight formations like American Fortresses and Liberators. We used to say that the only resemblance to formation flying by Lancasters and Halifaxes was that they were going in the same direction on the same day! Always there were one or two, for reasons best known to themselves, flying on their own several miles away from the main formation.

'Although I did not come into combat with Me109s and FW190s in a Mustang, I understand that it could more than hold its own with these enemy aircraft. My experience against Me262 jets, which had a much higher top speed than a Mustang, was that unless one had a height advantage of several thousand feet it was impossible to engage them. Manoeuvrability in those circumstances did not count a lot.

'My most memorable experience involving the Me262 occurred during an escort mission with over 450 RAF heavies to Hamburg on 31 March 1945, attacking the Blohm & Voss U-boat building yards.

'South of the target I noticed some vapour trails several thousand feet above us going in the same direction. I reported these to the CO who said they were probably Mosquito Pathfinders, but to keep an eye on them. Shortly afterwards I observed several Me262s diving through our formation from above and behind, travelling at high speed. We dropped our tanks and dived after the 262s, but before getting within range they opened fire on the leading bombers with what looked like rocket projectiles and cannon, scoring hits on at least two of the bombers. One of the 262s, breaking away from the attack, came back under us and Red Section, led by the CO, turned on our backs and went straight down after him at high speed. We opened fire at extreme range before he pulled away with his superior speed. In chasing the 262 I had to apply full rudder trim because of the high speed, and in climbing back over the bombers I was not quick enough in taking off the trim and as I lost speed my aircraft flicked into a violent spin. I lost several thousand feet before regaining control, by which time I had lost the protection of the "Window" being dropped by the bombers, and received the full attention of the radar-predicted anti-aircraft gunfire which prompted me to climb back as quickly as possible. By sheer luck I climbed back straight into formation with my CO, who was not at all pleased at losing his No 2 (it being an unforgivable sin for a No 2 to lose his leader, however briefly).

'Our wave of bombers was not attacked again by fighters, although we were plastered from ground fire. I understand that on that mission the bomber stream as a whole was attacked by about 30 Me262s and a number of FW190s. Eight Lancasters and three Halifaxes failed to return for whatever reason, assessed by Bomber Command as seven shot down by fighters, two by flak and two lost in a collision.'

The Mustang's range capability made it a valuable aircraft in the China-Burma-India (CBI) theatre where often vast distances had to be covered to

Above:
Lt A. X. Hiltgen and his crew chief, Sgt James Webb, on the wing of their P-51B. A. Hiltgen

reach enemy installations. By 1945 it was the predominant Allied type operating in China — over 350. 'Ax' Hiltgen was a pilot with one of the most successful Mustang squadrons:

'I was a pilot in the 530th Fighter Squadron (Yellow Scorpions) of the 311th Fighter Group. This group was formed in mid-1942 and after several moves trained as an operational unit with A-36s and P-51As and went to the China-Burma-India theatre in July 1943, taking its planes overseas on a

carrier. Our group was the first one in the theatre with the Mustang. We arrived in Assam, India, in September and flew our first combat missions in early October. Although the group remained in Assam, our squadron operated from Dacca, Dohazari and Ramu, in the Calcutta and Chittagong area. In India and Burma 60% of our missions were ground support, 20% escort of bombers or transports and 20% fighter sweeps for air superiority. We replaced our P-51As with P-51Cs (Merlin engine) in August of 1944 and the group moved to China the same month. In China the missions were 10% escort and 90% fighter sweeps to destroy either enemy aircraft or ground transport. The rate of operations in 1944 and early 1945 varied, depending on weather and squadron location. We had a forward base at Hsian and when the squadron was there 16 to 20 sorties were scheduled daily. However, we rotated with the other two squadrons back to Chengtu where we escorted B-29s coming back from Japan and did reconnaissance missions. The rate here would average four to eight per day. Weather at Hsian was definitely a factor in the winter months. Navigational aids were few to none and low cloud or snow would halt operations. Surprisingly, runways in China were good and far better than the ones we operated on in Burma and India. The runways at Dohazari and Ramu were grass in good weather and swamps in bad. In Burma we had a gravel strip that was tough all the time. In China all the runways we used were long and paved.

'From the time of our arrival in the CBI until the war's end our squadron destroyed 261 Japanese aircraft and probably destroyed another 114. In addition we were credited with destroying 532 locomotives, dropping 630 tons of bombs and expending close to 600,000 rounds of 0.50 calibre ammunition.

'The greatest problem we had with our first P-51Cs was bad seals in the prop allowing oil to spray over the canopy and windscreen making flying hazardous and landing one step short of panic. There is on record a case where four of our planes returning from a fighter sweep in China encountered a flight of Japanese training planes with fixed landing gear. Those of our people with ammunition couldn't see through the windscreen and therefore couldn't use the gunsight. They solved the problem by throttling back and putting their heads out of the side panels to shoot four of the planes down. This was the only real problem with the Merlin-powered Mustang and was solved when proper replacement parts were obtained.

'The two major advantages of these aircraft were altitude and range. In

Continued on page 58

Right:
Hiltgen's yellow-nosed *Al's Sylvia Gal*. A. Hiltgen

P-51s in Italy

Above:
Mustang units operating in Italy mostly had to operate from 'dirt' airfields with primitive facilities. Major maintenance often had to be carried out in the open and up-wind from the runway to avoid summer dust. Despite the sunshine it was not the most desirable location for an engine change. This No 260 Squadron Mk III was photographed at Termili in the summer of 1944. R. V. Palmer

Left and below:
The four US 15th Air Force Mustang fighter groups had red noses, this being a theatre marking for Allied fighter aircraft in Italy, although not adhered to by all units. Tail colours identified individual groups. Left: All-red tails marked the USAAF's only negro-manned fighter group, the 332nd. Below: Red tail stripes were used by the 31st, which had been in action longer than any other US fighter group in Europe. This is commanding officer Col William Daniel's P-51D under repair at Foggia Macu. USAAF/S. Staples

Top:
Most striking tail-marking was the black and yellow checkerboard identifying 325th Fighter Group. P-51C *Lady Jean* had — in the slang of the time — her ass chewed up.

Above:
The RAF's No 112 Squadron displayed its famous 'shark nose' on Mustang IVAs. Both USAAF and RAF Mustang units in Italy used US-supplied 75 and 110gal tanks. Only 130 grade fuel was used. Via B. Robertson

P-51s in China

Above:
Late-production P-51Ds and Ks had a new design of canopy. This resulted from pilot complaints about distortion of vision directly above and to the rear with the original 'bubble' canopy. The new model could be distinguished by the more bulged dome as on these two P-51-25-NAs of 76th Fighter Squadron at Luliang, China. G. Moriea

Right:
P-51s operating in China had the MN-26C radio compass set to aid navigation over areas where military homing beacons were few and far between. Most aircraft had the familiar ring aerial exposed but this 118th Tactical Reconnaissance (Tac Recon) Squadron F-6D sports a faired covering. G. Moriea

Above:
A Japanese air raid on Chengtu airfield riddled this new P-51C with bomb fragments. The wreck remained for months as a source of parts to keep other Mustangs serviceable.
B. Simpronio

Below:
Japanese airfields in China were well defended. Lt L. B. Corfman of 530th

Fighter Squadron brought his P-51C back to base after a shell had removed a large part of the right horizontal stabiliser.   B. Simpronio

Below right:
Speaking about another narrow escape, 'Barry' Corfman commented: 'I got jumped by a "Tojo" Mk 4 while on the deck strafing a locomotive — don't know what happened to my top cover at

10,000ft. To save my hide I went through the "War Emergency" safety wire and held the high blower switch in "High" position. The Rolls drew 96in of mercury for 4.5min and got me away from that Jap doing "Lazy Eights" on my ass. I got out of that with only a few holes and when my crew chief checked the oil cuno strainer he could find no metal in it. Now that's a strong engine!'   B. Simpronio

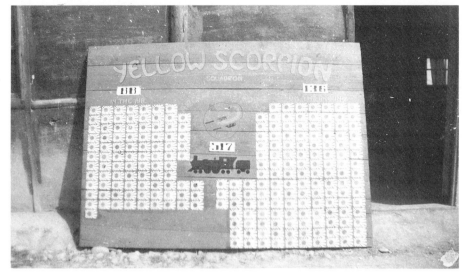

Left:
Scoreboard of the 530th Fighter Squadron with 88 air and 136 ground credits against aircraft, and 517 successful attacks on trains.
B. Simpronio

November 1943 we flew the longest fighter missions to that date with P-51As, close to 700 miles each way. We had to use full throttle only when absolutely necessary in the dogfight to conserve fuel to reach home and even then landed with nothing but fumes. With the P-51C this was a breeze and our primary concern was calloused posteriors. Altitude was important to get over the bad weather in combat and when we encountered "Tonys" and "Tojos" — particularly the latter. During combat with "Zeros" and "Oscars" it was a matter of keeping your speed up and not getting sucked into tight manoeuvres. As to maintenance, our squadron was outstanding in this regard, keeping an average of 96%-plus in commission rate, which I believe held for the "As", "Cs", plus the "Ds" after I left. The operating environment went from hot and humid in India and Burma to cold in China. Refuelling and rearming problems were no different and each

climate had its offsetting advantages and disadvantages.

'Our typical mission changed from India and Burma, from ground support of infantry to fighter sweeps. For escort of bombers, it was always maximum effort with 20 to 24 fighters and altitude in the 20,000-30,000ft range with distances of 500-800 miles. At this altitude the "A" would hang on the prop, but the "C" would match or exceed anything the Japanese had. Fortunately for us, as the Japanese planes got better — with the "Tojo" the best — their fighter pilot quality plummeted. On fighter sweeps in China we would always be in flights of eight or more. Half would stay at altitude for top cover and the others strafe rolling stock or airfields. On both escort and fighter sweeps the navigation radio and cockpit comfort of the P-51C was superior. With the "A" and the A-36 in India, a frequent problem was coolant temperature control where we had to operate the scoop

manually, but with the "C" this was non-existent.

'With pilots of equal ability the Mustang could whip any US fighter with perhaps the Corsair being, at best, a draw. This applied to all models of the P-51 and, if you stayed below 10,000ft, with with the A-36 as well. The climb rate, acceleration, turning radius and stability at all speeds and altitudes were superior in the Mustang. The only negative flying characteristic of the Merlin-powered Mustang was that with a full fuselage tank the plane would "porpoise" in tight turns. However, procedures called for using fuselage fuel first which corrected the centre of gravity problem.

'As mentioned earlier, the only Japanese plane that came close to the P-51 in speed, ceiling and flying characteristics was the "Tojo". With the "Oscar" and "Zero", if you stayed out of tight, slow manoeuvres and used the advantages of the Mustang you would win. In this comparison our Intelligence people briefed us on our first long range escort mission (Rangoon) that the Japanese pilots did not have parachutes. My first kill on this mission resulted in the pilot

Below:
P-51Cs resplendent in the yellow and black markings of 530th Fighter Squadron stand ready on Chengtu airfield for an escort mission.
B. Simpronio

FINAL MISSION REPORT

1. 506th Fighter Group, APO #86.
   Mission Leader: Major Malcolm C. Watters, 0 432 241

2. a. VLR Fighter Strike against Akenogahara and Suzuka A/Fs.
   b. 16 July 45   c. FO #146   d. Mission #07-12

3. a. Squadron

	457	458	462	Total
(1) A/C Dispatched	24	20	20	64
(2) Early Returns	2	4	2	8
(3) Sub Cover	2	0	2	4
(4) B-29 Cover	4	0	0	4
(5) Over Target	16	16	16	48
(6) A/C Lost	1	0	0	1
(7) Completed Mission	21	16	18	55

   b. Times:
   (1) T/O: 1025   (2) RV: 1045   (3) Landfall: 1335
   (4) Target: 1340-1440 (5) Landed: 1724

4. a. Our A/C Losses: 1
      Capt John W. L. Benbow 0 792 095, 457th Fighter Squadron. The flight
      of which Capt Benbow was a part became separated during aerial combat
      in the Suzuka Area. Pulling out of flying debris from a Jap plane
      destroyed in the fight caused his wingman to lose contact with his
      leader. Capt Benbow was not seen again and is considered missing.

   b. Our A/C Damaged: 1
      Capt Abner M. Aust 0 742 882, 457th Fighter Squadron. Damaged by
      enemy M/G fire. One 12.7 mm bullet entered upper right side of fuselage.
      In passing down and forward the slug destroyed DF and radio communications
      damaged two ribs, and on emerging peeled back two sections of the skin. The
      A second bullet struck the left gun bay cutting cable in the wing. The
      damage was inflicted by two Jap fighters making an overhead pass NW
      of Kumozu. Pilot uninjured.

5. a. Enemy A/C Sighted: 25-30 SE fighters in the area extending from the
      west shore of Ise Wan west to the center of the peninsula and from
      Nagoya on the north to Akenogahara on the south.

   b. Enemy A/C Losses: 10 destroyed, 1 probably destroyed, 9 damaged in the air
   (1) Destroyed -- Gp Hq -- Maj Malcolm C. Watters -- 1 Zeke
                    457th Ftr Sq -- Capt Abner M. Aust -- 2 SE UI
                                    1st Lt Wesley A. Murphey -- 1 Tojo

                                    Capt William B. Lawrence -- 1 SE UI

                    458th Ftr Sq -- Capt Richard W. Barnes -- 2 SE UI
                                    1st Lt Frank H. Wheeler -- 1 Frank

                    462nd Ftr Sq -- Capt Frederick A. Sullivan - 1 Zeke

                                    2nd Lt William J. Jutras -- 1 Zeke

CONFIDENTIAL

-1-

CONFIDENTIAL

(Mission Report #07-12 cont'd)

   (2) Probably destroyed:
          462nd Ftr Sq -- 1st Lt. Gordon C. Dingee -- 1 Frank

   (3) Damaged:

          Gp Hq -- Maj. Malcolm C. Watters -- 1 Zeke

          457th Ftr Sq -- Capt. Abner M. Aust -- 2 S/E UI
                          1st Lt. Thomas V. Carroll -- 1 S/E UI
                          1st Lt. Wesley A. Murphy -- 1 Zeke
                          2nd Lt. Thomas O. Wessall -- 1 S/E UI

          462nd Ftr Sq -- Capt. Fredrick A. Sullivan -- 1 Zeke
                          1st Lt. Edward F. Balhorn -- 1 Zeke
                          2nd Lt. Allen F. Colley -- 1 Tojo

   * All claims are subject to revision based on gun camera film or
     other information presented at a later date.

6. NARRATIVE: The mission was diverted from the planned fighter strike due
   to the presence of E/A in numbers airborne in the target area.
   The trip to DP was accomplished without incident. Landfall was made
   at about 15000' and the Group proceeded northward on a course calculated to
   parallel the west side of Ise Wan inshore. Between Akenogahara and Tsu
   bogies were called and soon thereafter all three Squadrons were engaged in
   a running air fight. The 457th Squadron in the lead ducked under a cloud and
   came upon what was described as a dogfight between a number of the enemy
   and members of the 21st Group. Our forces joined the engagement which followed the pattern of searching the area and attacking the enemy whenever
   the occasion presented itself. The enemy generally was unaggressive although
   some attempted to fight back when caught and attacked. The exception was an
   overhead attack by two Japs on Capt. Aust of the 457th while he was engaged
   in pursuing another E/A and a head on pass at short range by 2 of a group of
   Zekes which were painted earth brown on top and a darker brown underneath.
   Capt. Aust flamed one of these and then hit another so badly the pilot bailed
   out. The usual Jap evasive tactic was a split S into the cloud below at 6-
   8000'. A plan used successfully by Capt. Barnes of the 458th who destroyed 2
   was to circle above a hole in the cloud which the enemy could be expected
   to use in climbing through the overcast.
   Capt. Lawrence leading Green Flight of the 457th west of Akenogahara
   pulled on the tail of an E/A in an easy turn to the right at 15000'. He
   opened fire in range and followed the Jap in a split S. The enemy smoked and
   began to disintegrate. Capt. Benbow, Green #3 called on the radio 'That's
   enough Bill, you've got him'. Lt. Winn, Green #4, by this time was flying
   through so much debris he was forced to pull off temporarily losing his
   leader, Capt. Benbow. Capt. Benbow was not seen again. About that time and
   in the same general area what was believed to be a P-51 was observed by another
   flight apparently in trouble going down in slow gliding turns at an estimated
   150 MPH. This A/C disappeared into the clouds at about 8000'. The time was

CONFIDENTIAL

CONFIDENTIAL

(Final Mission Report #07-12 Cont'd)

reported 1350. Still another flight reported seeing one white parachute des-
cending in the same general area at 1355. It is possible Capt Benbow's plane
was damaged by pieces of the A/C shot down by Capt Lawrence. He was not known
to be under fire from the ground or air.
   The flight led by Maj Chapman jumped a single E/A. He scored hits followed
by Lt Wheeler and Capt Conner who also connected. The kill was awarded to
Wheeler who was acknowledged to have put in the most effective burst. This
A/C crashed near Suzuka A/F.
   The Japs were parachuting rather freely with three bailouts being reported
while the enemy was under attack and other open parachutes being noted which
were thought to be Japanese. Some were reported as khaki color.

7. FLAK:
   From the west shore of Ise Wan generally meager, heavy, inaccurate.
   8/10 overcast in the target area made visual gun laying impossible.

8. IMPORTANT OBSERVATIONS:
   a. Three Tojos were sighted without camouflage which is a departure from
      Jap practice previously observed.
   b. Akenogahara A/F was observed by several pilots all reporting no A/C
      visible from altitude.
   c. A few scattered A/C were seen on Suzuka A/F but they probably were
      dummies seen there previously.

9. Communications: Loud and Clear except with Doctor #1.

10. Weather:
    Iwo to 32° N -- 3/10 cirrus near 30000' and 3/10 cumulus based near 2000'
                    with tops at 4000' to 5000'. Visibility 50 miles.
    32° N to Coast -- 8/10 cirrostratus near 30000' and 4/10 cumulus based
                      near 2000' with tops at 5000' and few tops to 8000'.
                      Visibility 25 miles.
    Target Area -- 10/10 cirrostratus near 27000', 3/10 thin altostratus
                   near 17000', 3/10 thin altostratus near 14000', and 8/10
                   cumulus based at 5000' with tops at 8000'. Visibility
                   20 miles above lower clouds. Lowering to 5 miles in haze
                   beneath lower clouds. Frontal activity appeared to north-
                   east of target.

11. a. Ammunition expended.

        457th   6602
        458th   3256
        462nd   6750
                16608 rds. cal. .50

    b. Gas consumption:

	457	458	462	Sub Cover	B-29 Cover
Avg. gal. remaining	73	73	85		
Least remaining	60	50	80	127	74
Most remaining	94	110	116	160	92

CONFIDENTIAL
-3-

CONFIDENTIAL

(Final Mission Report #07-12 Cont'd)

12. REMARKS:
    a. The situation was complicated by the presence of a large number of A/C
       in a limited air space. It is believed the results would have been more
       decisive if there had not been as many friendly A/C helping out.
    b. It is believed more air contact with the enemy would result if fighter
       sweeps were authorized with strikes being made as a last resort in the
       event no air opposition materialized by the time the gas supply indicated
       a return to base. And then only after reconnaissance shows A/C on the
       field to provide suitable targets. By definitely committing the Group
       to a ground target in advance accomplishment of that mission inevitably
       detracts from the extent and effectiveness of the air search. Under
       the existing ground situation any aerial interception seems more likely
       to produce results in E/A destroyed. Finding targets on predetermined
       A/Fs under present conditions is a matter of chance. An opportunity to
       sweep the air uncommitted while searching the ground for a last resort
       target offers increased probability of joining action with the enemy's
       air forces.

                                        J. W. GILES,
                                        Major, Air Corps,
                                        S-2.

CONFIDENTIAL

-4-

HQS VII FC
IWO JIMA
1000K, 15 July 45

ANNEX "B" to FO No. 146.

NAVIGATION PLAN FOR 506TH FIGHTER GROUP

1. Take-off: As ordered by Group Commander.

    a. Magnetic course 359° to Rendezvous.

    b. Distance 39 nautical miles.

    c. Estimated time enroute 13 minutes (185 I.A.S. Climb to 10,000 ft).

2. Rendezvous KITA JIMA (25/25N - 141/17E):

    a. Leave Rendezvous by 0645 KING.

    b. Navigation B-29's at 10,000 feet altitude.

    c. 506th Fighter Group: 500 feet below B-29's.

3. Rendezvous to Departure Point (34/15N - 136/28E):

    a. Magnetic course 334°.

    b. Distance 586 nautical miles.

    c. Estimated time enroute 2 hours 49 minutes (205 I.A.S. @ 10,000 ft).

    d. Arrival time 0934 KING at D.P.

4. Departure Point to Primary Target (34/32N - 136/40E):

    a. Magnetic course 40°.

    b. Distance 22 nautical miles.

    c. Estimated time enroute 5 minutes (250 I.A.S. Letdown.).

    d. Arrival time 0939 KING at AKENOGAHARA Airfield.

5. Primary Target to Secondary Target (34/51N - 136/35E):

    a. Magnetic course 335°.

    b. Distance 15 nautical miles.

- 1 -

506th Gp - Nav Plan   S E C R E T

6. Primary Target to Rally Point (34/30N - 137/35E):

    a. Magnetic course 104°.

    b. Distance 45 nautical miles.

    c. Estimated time enroute 12 minutes (220 I.A.S. Climb to 10,000 ft).

    d. Navigation B-29's at 10,000 feet altitude.

    e. 506th Fighter Group: 500 feet below B-29's.

    f. 21st Fighter Group: 500 feet above B-29's.

7. Rally Point to Iwo Jima (24/47N - 141/17E):

    a. Magnetic course 170°.

    b. Distance 616 nautical miles.

    c. Estimated time enroute 2 hours 57 minutes (210 I.A.S. @ 10,000 ft).

    d. Estimated time of arrival 1328 KING.

NOTE: Route times based on forecast wind: 230° - 18 knots @ 10,000 ft.

OFFICIAL:

K. EMPFER
LT COL
COMBAT OPS O.

MOORE
BRIG GEN

- 2 -

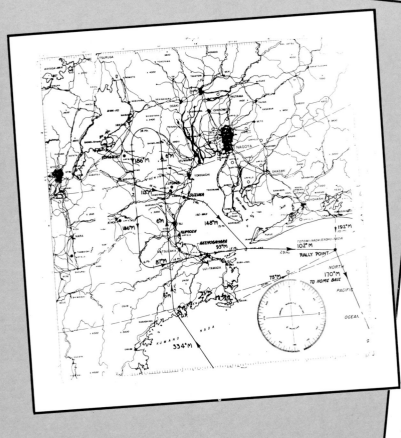

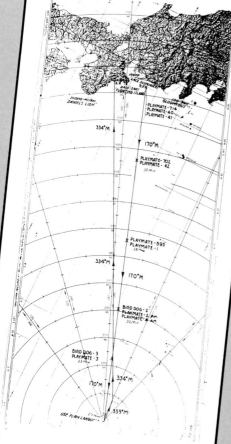

Navigation plans for 506th Fighter Group

baling out! They said that the Jap pilot would not make head-on passes. One of our pilots had his windscreen shot out with a head-on pass and he did the "chicken" turn. They also said the Japanese planes did not have armour plate for the pilot. An "Oscar" we shot down had half-inch steel behind and under the seat; the Mustang had quarter-inch and only behind the pilot.

'Summarising comparative characteristics, the Mustang was the best fighter; the Merlin-powered Mustangs gave us ceiling to get over weather, range for longer missions, better cockpit comfort and navigation. The one weak point on ground attacks was the radiator and I think 90% of the planes we lost on air-to-ground missions were lost through a hit in the radiator.

'Our squadron name, Yellow Scorpions, was given to us by Tokyo Rose, the girl who broadcast Jap propaganda in English. Being the first Mustang group in the CBI, and as our squadron selected to be the one detached to other units, we encountered more air-to-air combat. We had painted our spinners brilliant yellow. After a series of very successful fighter sweeps in the Mandalay area we heard Tokyo Rose report that "The Imperial Japanese Air Force annihilated the Yellow Scorpions of the US Air Force". In fact, we had shot down 25 Japanese aircraft in three days at a cost of five hits on one plane, and that was repaired in two hours. On the head-on pass mentioned earlier, the windscreen was completely shot out and the gunsight stopped the bullet, but it was blown back into the pilot's chest and he returned with it in his lap. Another pilot returned with 58 holes in his plane with cables severed and the plane flew again one week later. I returned with a cannon shell in the right fuel tank and 16in of one of the prop blades shot off.'

Mustang operations in the Pacific Ocean area were particularly notable for the vast distances involved in reaching objectives. Missions taking seven hours and covering 1,300 miles were the norm for the three P-51 Mustang fighter groups operating from Iwo Jima against the Japanese home islands. Edward Bahlhorn was one of the pilots:

'The 506th Fighter Group was formed in November 1944 using a large number of pilots who had previously served as instructors in P-39s and P-40s. We staged out of Lakeland, Florida, and included in our training were the rudiments of cruise control for very long range escort missions. When I first stepped into a P-51 I had over 600 hours in Allison-powered P-39s and P-40s, plus a few hours in the R-2800-powered P-47G. In my

opinion none of these aircraft could compete with the Merlin P-51 at any altitude; but it was above 20,000ft that it really excelled. I once tried to see how high I could go in a P-51D. The aircraft was perfectly tuned and after much coaxing I topped out 500ft above the listed service ceiling of 41,900ft. The last 2,000ft came very slowly and I had to "porpoise" to the point where the plane was literally hanging on the prop, mushing along. I guess it didn't prove anything but it gave me a satisfied feeling of accomplishment.

'We trained in the P-51A, B, C, D and K models and then received new P-51D-20s which we took to Guam on the USS *Kalinin Bay*, a jeep carrier. From Guam we flew them the 820 miles to the small island of Iwo Jima which had been wrested from the Japs at great cost in lives, primarily to provide a base for fighters to escort the B-29 raids and give a closer haven for combat-damaged bombers. With the exception of the first few, most of our missions were fighter strikes at airfields and targets of opportunity in Japan, as the B-29s reverted to night bombing. On fighter strikes our group had two squadrons go in on strafing runs while the third remained at altitude as top cover. Needless to say, ground strafing was not our favourite type of mission; however it was apparently something that had to be done. My only aerial encounter with a "Zero" was short-lived as we were on top of a low overcast when I spotted him and gave chase. I jettisoned my external tanks and immediately experienced engine failure — I had

Below:
Edward Bahlhorn (extreme right of picture) and some fellow pilots of 462nd Fighter Squadron in front of his P-51D *Meatball*. E. Bahlhorn

forgotten to change my fuel selector switch to an internal tank! This was quickly corrected and, although at maximum range, I opened fire. He did a slow roll and dove into the overcast. Not being at a very high altitude and not knowing the terrain under the overcast, I did not follow. However, I had observed some strikes on the enemy aircraft prior to losing it in the clouds. There had been no need to go through the gate to War Emergency Power as I was slowly gaining on him with 61in manifold pressure before I lost him.

'On these average 1,400-mile flights to and from Japan there was little relief from discomfort and boredom, especially on the return leg to Iwo. However, being short I would periodically raise my seat, then slouch down, place my feet on the cowling above the instrument panel and fly by stick only.

'The only drawback of the P-51, as with all aircraft with liquid-cooled engines, was the vulnerability of its coolant lines and radiator which, if hit, meant — in our case — a bath in the shark-infested Pacific. On one mission I became separated from my wingman and while returning to the rally point I came up with one of our squadron's planes and noticed it was losing coolant. Calling the pilot over the radio I then took his wing position. He advised me his coolant temperature was off the peg and that his engine was running very rough. The engine seized just after we made the enemy coastline and he had to bale out. His 'chute opened and when he hit the water he was able to inflate his dinghy and release sea marker dye. Meanwhile I circled the location calling "Playmate" over the radio to alert the rescue services. Then I realised I was alone and became concerned about fuel and my ability to find Iwo, some 600 miles away. This prompted me to call in the blind, advising there was a chick that needed assistance in returning home. My calls were answered, for a multi-engined Navy aircraft established radio contact and soon arrived to take over the orbit and direct the rescue submarine to the spot. As I was about to set course for Iwo a B-29 appeared — a beautiful sight — and navigated me home. The downed P-51 pilot, John Freeman, was saved, although I did not meet him again until well after the war.'

The planning and execution of a Mustang mission from Iwo Jima is presented in the following reproduction of the actual documents prepared by USAAF Intelligence Officers on Iwo Jima. KING times are Greenwich Mean Times. Bird-dog and Playmate are callsigns for lifeboat-carrying B-17s.

P-51s in Iwo Jima

Left:
The early missions flown by the first Mustangs to be based on Iwo were ground attack. These 47th Fighter Squadron P-51Ds are carrying 500lb bombs to attack Japanese strongholds on nearby islands.
Smithsonian Institution 64602AC

Below:
Although the likelihood of heavy Japanese air attack was remote, there was no room on Iwo for dispersed aircraft standings. Mustangs were lined up, wingtip to wingtip, along the sides of the compacted 'dirt' runways. White-banded P-51Ds of 531st Fighter Squadron in the foreground carry 110 USgal drop tanks ready for a mission. The other two 21st Fighter Group squadrons are in the background.
Smithsonian Institution A70314AC

Above:
Pilots are in their cockpits and crew chiefs are in attendance as they wait for the signal to start engines to begin a very long range fighter mission to Japan. These 506th Group P-51Ds have been drawn up beside the runway head, line astern with flights side by side in the order that they will move out to take-off.
Smithsonian Institution 67997AC

Left:
Landing back from a seven-hour mission. In contrast to practice in Europe, the landing circuit is clockwise. Wider separation of individual aircraft touching down lessened the effects of dust disturbance.
Smithsonian Institution 67980AC

6
Air Combat Victories

Approximately 5,800 enemy aircraft were shot down by Mustangs during World War 2 and some 300 of the 3,750-odd pilots involved could be called 'aces'. An ace is a fighter pilot who has shot down five or more of the enemy, an unofficial accolade with origins in World War 1 air fighting.

All but a score of the Mustang aces fought in Europe, where two-thirds served with the US 8th Air Force. Top-scoring Mustang pilot was Maj George E. Preddy of the 352nd Fighter Group operating chiefly from Bodney, England. Preddy was officially credited with 23.83 victories, this total being 22 plus two each shared with another pilot and one shared with three pilots. Preddy had previously flown P-47s and obtained three victories with that type. He was killed by US ground fire while flying low over the frontline area in France on Christmas Day 1944. The next highest standing for a pilot flying a Mustang was that of another 352nd Group pilot, Lt-Col John C. Meyer. His 21 credits included two shared with other pilots. Like Preddy, Meyer had, additionally, three victories in P-47s. Also with 21 victories and heading the table of 15th Air Force fliers was Capt John J. Voll. He achieved his total in a five-month period during the second half of 1944 while flying with the 308th Fighter Squadron of the 31st Fighter Group.

The next placings were Maj Glenn T. Eagleston of 354th Fighter Group and Capt Leonard K. Carson of 357th Fighter Group, both with 18.50 credits. Eagleston was also the leading ace in the 9th Air Force, having flown two tours. Next to Carson in the 8th Air Force came Maj Ray S. Wetmore with 18 victories in Mustangs. He had previously been credited with 3.25 victories in P-47s. Second highest victory total in the Italian-based 15th Air Force was Capt James S. Varnell of the 2nd Fighter Squadron, 52nd Fighter Group. He shot down 17 enemy aircraft in just over two months of operations.

Because of the nature of their operational commitment, RAF Mustang pilots did not have the opportunity to achieve large personal scores with only six having ace status in the type. The distinguished Pole, Sqn Ldr E. Horbaczewski, had 5.5 victories credited while flying with No 315 Squadron. Sqn Ldr L. A. P. Burra-Robinson of No 65 Squadron had 5.25 credits. In common with the USAAF, the percentages indicated victories shared with other pilots. For a period during the summer of 1944, three RAF Mustang squadrons detailed to intercept V-1 flying bombs brought

Above:
Capt Glenn Eagleston — pictured here in November 1944 — was one of the original pilots of the first and most successful Merlin Mustang squadron, the 353rd. His 18½ victories total was the highest in the US 9th Air Force.
USAAF

Above:
Maj John Herbst, leading P-51 ace in the CBI Theatre of Operations.
Smithsonian Institution 55902AC

down nearly 200. In this respect the most successful pilot was Flg Off J. Hartley of No 129 Squadron, with 11 V-1 credits.

Against Japan, the Mustang squadrons operating in China were the most successful. Lt-Col John C. Herbst led the high credits with 17, achieved

Below:
Maj George 'Ratsy' Preddy — number one Mustang ace. USAAF

while flying with 74th and 76th Fighter Squadrons of the 23rd Fighter Group. Next highest total was that of Lt-Col Edward O. McComas, commanding the 118th Tactical Reconnaissance Squadron in the same group. His 14 victories were obtained in just two months, and on one mission he was credited with shooting down five Japanese fighters. Mustang-equipped fighter units operating in the Western Pacific war zones did not have frequent contact with the enemy and the most successful ace was Maj Robert W. Moore who shot down 11 while flying with the 45th and 78th Fighter Squadrons of the 15th Fighter Group. He had an earlier victory in a P-47.

In the later stages of hostilities, when the quality of both German and Japanese pilots had deteriorated through lack of experience and insufficient training, several Mustang pilots were able to make multiple 'kills' during a single sortie, achieving 'ace in a day' status. For Europe these were as follows:

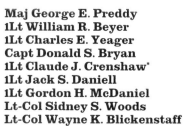

Above:
Capt Don Gentile of 336th Fighter Squadron was the first pilot to achieve considerable success flying a Merlin Mustang in air combat. An ex-RAF Eagle Squadron pilot, he was credited with 16 victories in the six weeks following his unit's conversion to the Mustang. USAAF

Maj George E. Preddy	487FS, 352FG	8AF	**6 e/a**	6 Aug 44
1Lt William R. Beyer	376FS, 361FG	8AF	**5 e/a**	27 Sep 44
1Lt Charles E. Yeager	363FS, 357FG	8AF	**5 e/a**	12 Oct 44
Capt Donald S. Bryan	328FS, 352FG	8AF	**5 e/a**	2 Nov 44
1Lt Claude J. Crenshaw*	369FS, 359FG	8AF	**5 e/a**	21 Nov 44
1Lt Jack S. Daniell	505FS, 339FG	8AF	**5 e/a**	26 Nov 44
1Lt Gordon H. McDaniel	318FS, 325FG	15AF	**5 e/a**	14 Mar 44
Lt-Col Sidney S. Woods	HQ 4FG	8AF	**5 e/a**	22 Mar 45
Lt-Col Wayne K. Blickenstaff	350FS, 353FG	8AF	**5 e/a**	24 Mar 45

(Note: *An official postwar survey only credits Crenshaw with four for this operation.)

Against the Japanese, in addition to McComas who shot down five of the enemy on 23 December 1944, the only other 'ace in a day' action was that of Capt William A. Shomo, commander of the 82nd Tactical Reconnaissance Squadron, 71st Reconnaissance Group. On 11 January 1945, while he and his wingman were on a scouting mission over Luzon, they were able to make a surprise attack on a lone bomber escorted by several fighters. In the confusion caused, Shomo not only despatched the bomber but six of the fighters. This action later brought him the Medal of Honor, highest US award for bravery.

The only other Mustang pilot to receive the Medal of Honor was Maj James H. Howard, commander of the 356th Fighter Squadron, 354th Fighter Group, a pioneer P-51B unit. The action took place exactly a year before Shomo's during a bomber escort over Germany where Howard single-handedly drove off repeated Luftwaffe attacks on a group of B-17s.

Left:
The only US pilot in Europe to be awarded his country's highest decoration for air combat action was Maj James Howard, CO of 356th Fighter Squadron. The Japanese 'kills' were obtained during earlier combat service, with the American Volunteer Group in China. His personal P-51B, 43-6315, had a Malcolm hood installed a few weeks after this picture was taken. USAAF

From the foregoing it will be seen that the pilots running up large totals of air victories were predominantly those of senior rank and in squadron or similar command positions. As squadron formation leaders they were in the position of deciding when to initiate an attack and were well placed to shoot down the enemy while still retaining surprise. Leading elements of a strike were always best placed for success. Whereas flight and element leaders would be detailed to fly different positions in a unit formation from mission to mission, the squadron commander would always be in the van. In most instances he was, of course, best suited to make a successful attack through his greater experience.

The most successful fighter squadron in terms of air victories, and also the top-scoring squadron in the USAAF, was the 353rd Fighter Squadron of the 354th Fighter Group. Assigned to the 9th Air Force, this unit was the first equipped with Merlin Mustangs in the United Kingdom and initially conducted operations in support of the 8th Air Force heavy bomber campaign. After D-day the unit moved to France, flying tactical fighter support missions until the end of hostilities. The 353rd FS was credited with a total 289.50 air victories, 276.50 while flying P-51s, the work of 84 individual pilots. The runner-up was the 8th Air Force's 364th Fighter Squadron of the 357th Fighter Group with 212 credits involving 70 pilots. Next came another 8th Air Force unit, the 487th Fighter Squadron of 352nd Fighter Group with 206 victories by 62 pilots. This squadron had previously destroyed 29 enemy aircraft while flying P-47s.

Below:
Luftwaffe crosses appeared on P-51s operating against the Japanese. Maj Walker Mahurin scored 20 victories flying P-47s in Europe before commanding the 3rd Air Commando Squadron in the SWPA where he added a single Japanese credit to the total. Mahurin also had victories in the Korean War. USAF

Mustang Pilot's Garb

Left:
Standing between his aircraft's ground staff, Flg Off Edward Roemmele of No 122 Squadron wears British Mae West sea life preserver over standard RAF battle dress. Oxford calf leather 'Escape boots' with black suede detachable tops. Leather flying gloves to protect hands in case of fire. The silk scarf prevented the neck chafing that could come from the constant head turning in watching for the enemy.
E. Roemmele

Below left:
Typical USAAF P-51 pilot flight clothes worn by Lt Henry Plunk of 436th Fighter Squadron. A leather AN-J-3 Intermediate Jacket is worn over AN-S-31 Summer Flying Suit. Popularly called 'coveralls', the suit was made of cotton twill. Gloves are carried in one of the two calf pockets and a clear plastic pocket has been added on the right thigh for positioning a flight data card. Plunk also wears a parachute silk scarf, which was not an official US issue.
USAAF

Below:
Lt Alvin Deeds of 350th Fighter Squadron sports alternative US American flight clothing. A B-15 jacket with mouton collar and A-11 trousers made from alpaca and wool pile material. He carries a RAF 'C' type flying helmet. The tinted flying goggles are type AN-6530. Deeds also has his back parachute and dinghy seat pack equipment attached. USAAF

7 Operational Modifications

The Mustang shipped to a theatre of war was not acceptable for combat by the operating air force without the aircraft undergoing a modification programme. Differing operational requirements and environments dictated changes to the standard production model which were carried out locally prior to the aircraft being delivered to a combat unit. Apart from the peculiar needs of the various air forces, most modifications were occasioned by operational experience when failures or weaknesses in the aircraft and its systems were brought to light.

Eventually many of these changes were made on the production line or, to prevent disruption of manufacture, a modification centre in the United States prior to overseas shipment.

The European Theatre of Operations embraced the largest force of Merlin Mustangs and developed the most comprehensive programme of Mustang modification. Operating agencies in other parts of the world did not enjoy the high standard of facilities available in the UK and modifications were generally performed at a lower level in the servicing establishment. The USAAF's Base Air Depot Area in the UK developed a listing of modifications and servicing requirements. First issued in November 1943 and periodically updated, this listing had covered more than 70 different items by the end of hostilities, although this was considerably less than for some other aircraft types. Many of these requirements were dropped when either incorporated in production or superseded by revisions. The most comprehensive listing of those issued was that of 5 August 1944 which gives a good indication of requirements and problems highlighted in nine months' operational use of Merlin Mustangs. Covering all model P-51s, this listing was divided into two stages: Stage I concerned items that had to be completed before an aircraft was passed as operational. Stage II listed high priority modifications considered absolutely necessary for combat operations and, if parts were available, to be carried out before an aircraft was reported operational. The availability of modification kits was the deciding factor.

STAGE I

Item 1
Form 1A inspection. (This was the normal pre-delivery check covering all aspects of airframe, engine and accessories.)

Item 2
Change boost control to provide 61in at gate and 67in through gate. (Manifold pressure into the engine cylinders, boosted by the supercharger blower, was measured by inches of mercury. The setting on the pilot's operating quadrant was at 61in for normal maximum power at the stop [gate], and for extra emergency power when the stop was bypassed to 67in.)

Item 4
Modification of the mixture control lever operation to eliminate FULL-RICH and AUTO-RICH positions (to prevent the lever being moved to a setting which would give these over-rich fuel mixture deemed unnecessary for European usage).

Item 5
Replacement of the enrichment jet and resetting of operating valve. (This referred to the water injection apparatus on the engine which allowed extra power to be drawn without damage to the combustion chambers. A smaller

Below:
The first P-51Bs to reach the squadrons had type recognition bands applied by hand brush. The bands were supposed to be applied at precise widths but, as can be seen, there was considerable variation. USAAF

valve was installed as the original was considered too generous for the higher air humidity of northern Europe, and could have an adverse effect on engine performance.)

Item 6
Aircraft markings. (The special type identity marking which consisted of a white spinner, noseband and a single stripe across each wing and tailplane surface on camouflaged aircraft, or black on those with bare metal finish. This was an aid to preventing confusion with enemy fighter types.)

Item 9
Pressurise 75 USgal combat wing tanks, except on tactical reconnaissance versions. (The means of pressurising jettisonable auxiliary fuel tanks had been developed by USAAF agencies in the UK by harnessing the exhaust of the instrument vacuum pump. This directive referred to making this installation if it had not been incorporated in production. Only early P-51B and C models arrived without this facility.)

Item 10
Rework or replacement of exhaust stacks. (In early operations it was found that many engine exhaust stacks developed serious cracks, presenting a fire hazard. Until stronger components became available the stacks were reinforced by welding a metal strip on each side.)

Item 11
Inspect empennage attachment bolts. (Following several fatal accidents where tail components had come away in flight, P-51Bs were temporarily grounded in February 1944. Inspections revealed that bolts holding the tail were in many cases improperly tightened and often of insufficient length to allow proper tightening. Although the embargo lasted for only a few days, all new P-51s continued to be checked in this respect.)

Item 12
Full power check. (To ascertain that the engine was delivering the required power at various control settings. While matter-of-course procedure, many early P-51Bs and Cs had been found to have considerable power variations on the original factory settings.)

Item 13
Swing compass. (The procedure for setting up an accurate compass reading was common to all aircraft. This requirement was actually the last to be performed before the Mustang was ready for delivery to a tactical unit — despite the position in this listing.)

Item 14
Reinforcement of horizontal stabiliser. (The stresses that high speeds and uncautioned handling produced in Merlin Mustangs soon highlighted a weakness in the tailplane which showed up as bending and, in a few instances, complete failure. A doubler plate was produced for reinforcement of the tailplane spar until a strengthened component could be incorporated during production.)

Item 15
Inspection of engine mounting bolts and nuts. (Another check arising from a number of accidents early in 1944 featuring the separation of the engine from the airframe during pull-outs or sharp manoeuvres. It was found that the engine mounting bolts and nuts for use on early P-51Bs were insufficiently robust to retain the Merlin engine. Replacement by more substantial, high tensile bolts and nuts proved the answer.)

Item 17
Install zerk fitting on coolant pump. (Engine coolant pump bearings were more durable when a nipple fitting was provided for greasing.)

Item 19
Removal of bomb racks on tactical reconnaissance aircraft only. (As the internal tankage of a Mustang was quite sufficient for the usual battle area tactical reconnaissance missions, the wing pylon bomb and drop-tank holding racks were considered restrictive through their weight and drag.)

Item 20
Replacement of left aileron counterbalance assembly. (Found unsatisfactory and modified.)

Item 21
Inspection and rework of coolant header tank scroll tubes. (The internal tubing assembly in the coolant header tank cracked, causing it to vibrate and wear a hole through the tank wall with subsequent loss of coolant. The original measures in reworking the header tank to strengthen this component also proved to be insufficiently strong. Cracking of the scroll tubes was a recurrent problem that persisted to the end of hostilities and was not banished until a new, stronger

Above:
Servicing the radio and dynamotor behind the armoured seat could only be done with great difficulty. USAAF

design of tank was forthcoming from the United States.)

Item 22
Modification of the supercharger volute drain valve assemblies. (A change made to improve the ease of servicing.)

Item 23
Rework of generator conduit. (The wiring harness of the electrical generator was found to impede some servicing tasks and was also exposed to damage.)

Item 24
Reposition of SCR-522 radio, battery and dynamotor. (To service the dynamotor the armoured pilot's seat had to be removed, a task requiring considerable time. The repositioning changes were made so that the dynamotor was accessible for service without removing the seat.)

Item 25
Remove the first aid kit. (Installed behind and above the seat by the manufacturer, it was deemed unnecessary as all pilots carried a first aid kit in their personal equipment.)

Item 26
Installation of sway brace for 108 USgal wing tanks. (These British-made impregnated paper or steel tanks required a special brace to prevent oscillation on the wing racks.)

(Note: *The numbered items missing from this listing were those only applicable to the P-51A and A-36A [Allison-engined versions] or requirements that had been superseded.*)

Above:
A familiar sight at Mustang dispersals: a pile of silver-doped red-banded 108gal paper-plastic composition tanks, manufactured by the Bowater Co in the UK. This is a 434th Fighter Squadron dispersal at Wattisham.

Above:
A frequent chore: SSgt Harry East tightens coolant line clamps on a 336th Fighter Squadron P-51B. The first thing a crew chief did on arriving at his aircraft in the morning was to check under the engine for coolant leaks. IWM EA18953

Below:
The so-called 'paper tank' which became the standard type used by UK-based Mustangs during the final months of the war in Europe. Rated as 108 USgal capacity, it had the advantage of being strong but light — easily lifted by one man. Two of these tanks allowed this 357th Group Mustang to fly 1,500 miles to Russia. USAAF

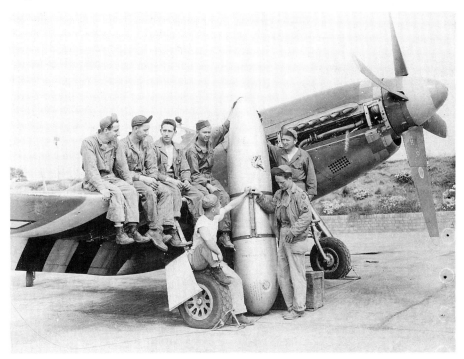

Above:
The two-seat adaptation made by 4th Fighter Group to war-weary P-51B 43-12193. Conversions were mostly carried out by individual group engineering establishments. Construction varied with a score of different hood arrangements among some 40 two-seat Mustangs. P. Betz

Above:
To aid identification of the formation leader at night or in bad weather, some Mustang units installed coloured lights in the fuselage sides of leader's aircraft. On this 357th Fighter Group P-51D-20-NA — personal aircraft of Lt-Col Andy Evans — two such lights can be seen, one forward of the victory display and the other in the centre of the national insignia. USAAF

STAGE II

Item 1

Downward identification lights. (The original wing leading edge light covers cracked through the slight flexing of wings during combat manoeuvres. These covers were removed and faired over with metal, the lights being repositioned in the under surfaces of the wings. In this position they were clearly visible from the ground and could be used to flash signals.)

Item 3

Installation of sliding hood. (The so-called Malcolm hood designed and manufactured for the RAF by a British company proved a vast improvement over the restricted vision of the original P-51B and C cockpit canopy. Demand for these bulbous one-piece canopies was greater than the manufacturers could meet during the first nine months of Merlin Mustang service, and numbers acquired by USAAF units were small. Priority was given to the tactical reconnaissance aircraft of the 9th Air Force, initially the 67th Reconnaissance Group and the 363rd Reconnaissance Group, the majority of whose P-51Bs and Cs — and the true photographic versions, F-6B and F-6C — were equipped with these hoods. Practically all RAF Mustang IIIs were eventually modified to take these sliding hoods.)

Item 4

Installation of gun camera overrun control. (This allowed the wing-mounted camera to continue operating for selected time periods after the guns had ceased firing. Additional film footage provided for better assessment of target destruction.)

Item 5

Replacing operating solenoid on all 0.50 guns. (The G-9 type fitted to the P-47 guns were considered more reliable.)

Item 7

Installation of selective bomb release. (To enable a pilot to release the left or right bomb or drop tank individually. Later P-51Ds had this facility incorporated at the factory.)

Item 8

Rear-view mirror on bubble canopy. (With the provision of the all-round view canopy on the P-51D, rear-view mirrors were deemed no longer necessary by the factory. However, for a quick scan of the rear, combat pilots still found them invaluable and requested reinstatement. The mirrors were fixed to the framing of the windshield. However, in the Pacific war zones, many units fixed mirrors to the instrument shrouding inside the windshield on P-51Ds.)

Above:
An additional 'coffin hood' installed on a 78th Fighter Group two-seat conversion of P-51B 42-106826. Late in 1944 Mustang groups in Europe were given permission to convert two 'war-weary' P-51s each as two-seat operational trainers. At this time combat groups had been given the responsibility of providing operational training for newly assigned pilots. The conversions enabled experienced pilots more easily to teach the tricks of the trade in flying the P-51 in combat.
E. Meinke

Item 9

Reinforcement of the hydraulic hand pump mounting. (This hand pump operated flaps when the engine was not running. Situated to the right of the seat, the lever mounting failed in some aircraft when vigorous hand pumping took place.)

Item 10

Rework propellers due to oil leakage. (Early P-51B and C models had poor seals in the propeller mechanism which allowed oil to escape from the spinner, to be thrown over the engine cowling and sometimes on to the windshield, partly obscuring vision. This trouble did not affect all aircraft, but a programme of fitting better seals was undertaken.)

Item 11
Removal of carburettor heating system. (This applied only to the P-51C model and was found unnecessary.)

Item 12
Replacement of phenolic canopy guide blocks. (Found troublesome in opening and closing canopy.)

Item 13
Replace non-reinforced oxygen bottles with reinforced type. (Withstood higher pressures and gave added safety.)

Item 14
Rework coolant pump. (Improvements to increase the reliability of this unit.)

Item 15
Installation of BC-608 contactor unit. (For radio equipment.)

Item 16
Installation of safety bolts for canopy side panels. (The small panels of P-51B and C cockpit glazing, situated to the rear of the pilot's seat, were secured by spring clips. It was found these could become dislodged in flight, notably in turns and dives. To prevent their loss, a bolted assembly was fabricated to secure the panels.)

Item 17
Rework rigging and testing of bomb rack assembly. (Frequent reports of the release mechanism failing to work led to this receiving attention.)

Item 18
Fuel gauge reworked and modification of scupper at fuel tank vent outlet. (This referred to the rear fuselage tank where fuel was lost through the venting assembly.)

Although many of these requirements were deleted from later issues of the P-51 listing, several new ones were added. Notable were the installation of a landing gear handle protective guard, warning system for low oxygen pressure, a return to two-position mixture control, modifications to enable a higher octane 100/150 fuel to be used, installation of a bobweight assembly to the elevators, installation of a dorsal fin and rudder reverse boost tab, installation of an additional landing gear uplock, alterations to the pilot's seat and a quick-release for its detachment with the armour plate.

The landing gear handle guard was the result of a number of incidents where the handle had been inadvertently dislodged from the down position, causing the gear to retract and, if unnoticed by the pilot, a wheels-up arrival on the runway. A downwards movement of the handle lowered the undercarriage but it was necessary to pull the lever inwards to the locked position. This brought the

Above:
A P-38 Lightning mirror on the sliding canopy of 479th Fighter Group commander's P-51D (44-14327). Crew chief H. Leachman is in the cockpit. H. Leachman

Above right:
The single 'Spitfire' type on a 357th Fighter Group P-51B. Sgt Olmsted poses for camera. M. Olmsted

Right:
Lt-Col George Ceuleers' P-51D at 364th Fighter Group sports a single 'Spitfire' type. USAF

handle close to the pilot's left leg. The problem was first highlighted by RAF pilots who wore a long flying boot which tended to rub against the handle in the locked position without the wearer noticing, due to concentration on landing approach. The RAF quickly improvised a guard to avoid this danger and a variation of this was later adopted by the USAAF.

Concentration on combat flying, and a failure to monitor the oxygen instrumentation visually, led to the introduction of an audio warning to alert a pilot of the status of the oxygen system.

Operation of the mixture controls and changes for the use of 100/150 fuel was allied to an ongoing concern with engine operation. During the spring of 1944 selected 8th Air Force fighter groups ran a trial on the use of a higher octane fuel which permitted the use of higher manifold pressures to draw more power. Despite a definite

Above right:
Twin 'Spitfire' mirrors adorn Maj Joe Thury's P-51D, 44-14656 of 339th Fighter Group. USAF

Right:
In another variation, twin mirrors are mounted on each side of the windshield framing on Lt Don Kammer's 353rd Fighter Group P-51D 44-11155. D. Kammer

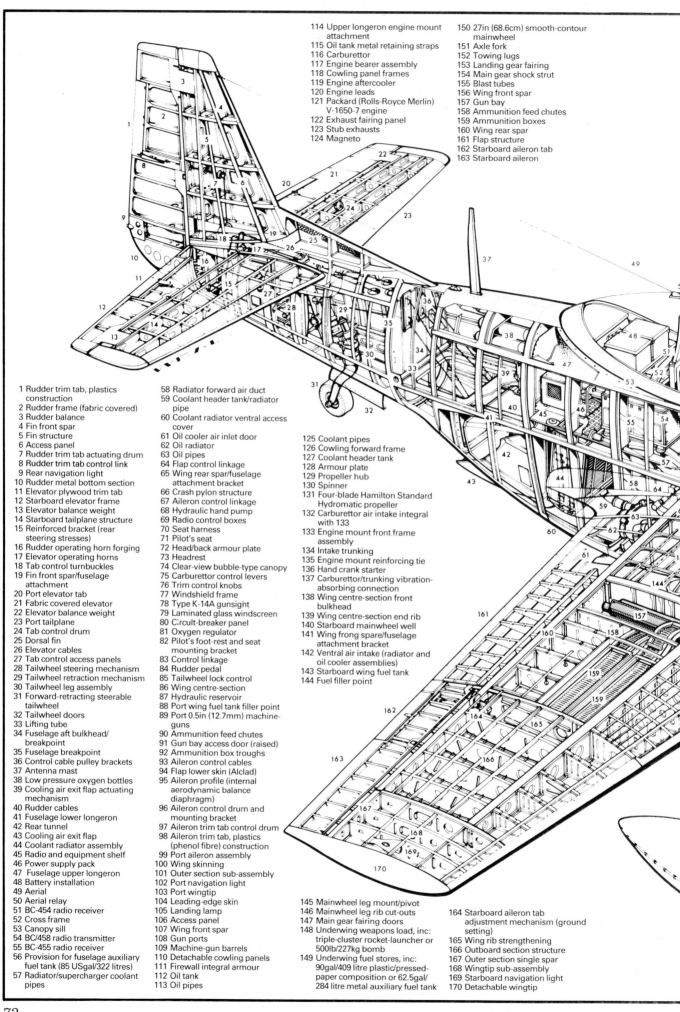

114 Upper longeron engine mount attachment
115 Oil tank metal retaining straps
116 Carburettor
117 Engine bearer assembly
118 Cowling panel frames
119 Engine aftercooler
120 Engine leads
121 Packard (Rolls-Royce Merlin) V-1650-7 engine
122 Exhaust fairing panel
123 Stub exhausts
124 Magneto

150 27in (68.6cm) smooth-contour mainwheel
151 Axle fork
152 Towing lugs
153 Landing gear fairing
154 Main gear shock strut
155 Blast tubes
156 Wing front spar
157 Gun bay
158 Ammunition feed chutes
159 Ammunition boxes
160 Wing rear spar
161 Flap structure
162 Starboard aileron tab
163 Starboard aileron

1 Rudder trim tab, plastics construction
2 Rudder frame (fabric covered)
3 Rudder balance
4 Fin front spar
5 Fin structure
6 Access panel
7 Rudder trim tab actuating drum
8 Rudder trim tab control link
9 Rear navigation light
10 Rudder metal bottom section
11 Elevator plywood trim tab
12 Starboard elevator frame
13 Elevator balance weight
14 Starboard tailplane structure
15 Reinforced bracket (rear steering stresses)
16 Rudder operating horn forging
17 Elevator operating horns
18 Tab control turnbuckles
19 Fin front spar/fuselage attachment
20 Port elevator tab
21 Fabric covered elevator
22 Elevator balance weight
23 Port tailplane
24 Tab control drum
25 Dorsal fin
26 Elevator cables
27 Tab control access panels
28 Tailwheel steering mechanism
29 Tailwheel retraction mechanism
30 Tailwheel leg assembly
31 Forward-retracting steerable tailwheel
32 Tailwheel doors
33 Lifting tube
34 Fuselage aft bulkhead/breakpoint
35 Fuselage breakpoint
36 Control cable pulley brackets
37 Antenna mast
38 Low pressure oxygen bottles
39 Cooling air exit flap actuating mechanism
40 Rudder cables
41 Fuselage lower longeron
42 Rear tunnel
43 Cooling air exit flap
44 Coolant radiator assembly
45 Radio and equipment shelf
46 Power supply pack
47 Fuselage upper longeron
48 Battery installation
49 Aerial
50 Aerial relay
51 BC-454 radio receiver
52 Cross frame
53 Canopy sill
54 BC/458 radio transmitter
55 BC-455 radio receiver
56 Provision for fuselage auxiliary fuel tank (85 USgal/322 litres)
57 Radiator/supercharger coolant pipes

58 Radiator forward air duct
59 Coolant header tank/radiator pipe
60 Coolant radiator ventral access cover
61 Oil cooler air inlet door
62 Oil radiator
63 Oil pipes
64 Flap control linkage
65 Wing rear spar/fuselage attachment bracket
66 Crash pylon structure
67 Aileron control linkage
68 Hydraulic hand pump
69 Radio control boxes
70 Seat harness
71 Pilot's seat
72 Head/back armour plate
73 Headrest
74 Clear-view bubble-type canopy
75 Carburettor control levers
76 Trim control knobs
77 Windshield frame
78 Type K-14A gunsight
79 Laminated glass windscreen
80 Circuit-breaker panel
81 Oxygen regulator
82 Pilot's foot-rest and seat mounting bracket
83 Control linkage
84 Rudder pedal
85 Tailwheel lock control
86 Wing centre-section
87 Hydraulic reservoir
88 Port wing fuel tank filler point
89 Port 0.5in (12.7mm) machine-guns
90 Ammunition feed chutes
91 Gun bay access door (raised)
92 Ammunition box troughs
93 Aileron control cables
94 Flap lower skin (Alclad)
95 Aileron profile (internal aerodynamic balance diaphragm)
96 Aileron control drum and mounting bracket
97 Aileron trim tab control drum
98 Aileron trim tab, plastics (phenol fibre) construction
99 Port aileron assembly
100 Wing skinning
101 Outer section sub-assembly
102 Port navigation light
103 Port wingtip
104 Leading-edge skin
105 Landing lamp
106 Access panel
107 Wing front spar
108 Gun ports
109 Machine-gun barrels
110 Detachable cowling panels
111 Firewall integral armour
112 Oil tank
113 Oil pipes

125 Coolant pipes
126 Cowling forward frame
127 Coolant header tank
128 Armour plate
129 Propeller hub
130 Spinner
131 Four-blade Hamilton Standard Hydromatic propeller
132 Carburettor air intake integral with 133
133 Engine mount front frame assembly
134 Intake trunking
135 Engine mount reinforcing tie
136 Hand crank starter
137 Carburettor/trunking vibration-absorbing connection
138 Wing centre-section front bulkhead
139 Wing centre-section end rib
140 Starboard mainwheel well
141 Wing frong spare/fuselage attachment bracket
142 Ventral air intake (radiator and oil cooler assemblies)
143 Starboard wing fuel tank
144 Fuel filler point

145 Mainwheel leg mount/pivot
146 Mainwheel leg rib cut-outs
147 Main gear fairing doors
148 Underwing weapons load, inc: triple-cluster rocket-launcher or 500lb/227kg bomb
149 Underwing fuel stores, inc: 90gal/409 litre plastic/pressed-paper composition or 62.5gal/284 litre metal auxiliary fuel tank

164 Starboard aileron tab adjustment mechanism (ground setting)
165 Wing rib strengthening
166 Outboard section structure
167 Outer section single spar
168 Wingtip sub-assembly
169 Starboard navigation light
170 Detachable wingtip

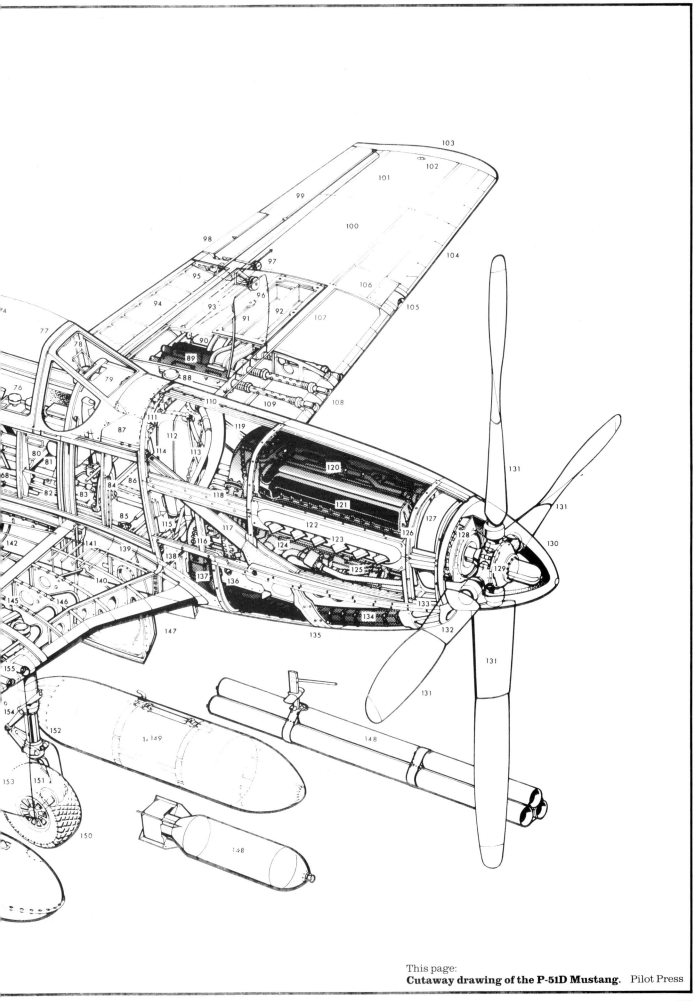

This page:
Cutaway drawing of the P-51D Mustang. Pilot Press

Above:
The location of the oil breather vent, on the right side of the engine cowling, exasperated many crew chiefs who endeavoured to keep their charges in pristine condition. Any surging of oil resulted in a discharge that ended as a plume swept back across the fuselage side and down on to the wing root and radiator housing. USAAF

tendency to increase spark plug fouling, all 8th Fighter Command P-51 groups changed over from 100/130 to 100/150 fuel that summer. During the autumn of 1944 there was a marked increase in the number of take-off crashes due to engine failure with the high octane fuel as the indirect main suspect. However, a detailed technical survey failed to pinpoint any one common cause of these accidents, finding that in most cases the crashes were probably due to uncautioned use of engine controls and failure to employ measures to minimise the risk of plug fouling during engine operation prior to take-off. Nevertheless, the high incidence of plug fouling brought the addition of ethylene dibromide to the 100/150 fuel to lessen plug carbonising. Tests were conducted by a P-51 group early in 1945 with satisfactory results. This fuel with additive, known as PEP, was

supplied to all USAAF fighter groups in the UK during February 1945. However, a new problem soon became evident in that valve seatings required frequent attention due to either stretching of the stems or a burning away of seating inserts. By April the position with valve clearance was so serious that inspections were advised after every 25 hours' flying. Moreover, burnt-out valve seating had become such a major cause of required engine changes that an acute shortage of replacement V-1650 Merlins arose. The average life of an engine was now reduced to under 100 hours. In an effort to overcome this crisis, a return to the 100/130 fuel was ordered, although initially there was some difficulty in arranging and sustaining the supply.

During the final months of hostilities in Europe the regular analysis of P-51 loss through mechanical and related failures continued. Despite all the concern over the high octane fuel problems, the analysis constantly showed the principal cause of loss to be through coolant failures. Coolant lines which ran from the engine to the radiator situated under the centre fuselage, included several hoses and gasket-type joints which required regular attention to prevent leaks. The efficiency of these joints was aggravated by the extremes in temperature encountered in Mustang operations. A

severe loss of coolant could quickly lead to engine overheating and seizure or detonation. There was another serious aspect to coolant leaks. The 70% ethylene glycol/30% water solution leaking at normal operating temperatures, gave off a toxic vapour which, if entering the cockpit, could have fatal consequences for a pilot. There were several reports of such leakage where pilots had later experienced severe stinging in the eyes, but there were also cases where inhalation of these vapours was believed to have caused 'drunken flying' precipitating a fatal crash.

The coolant system of the P-51 was most vulnerable during low-level flight over hostile defences where a lucky shot from a single rifle could hole a line or radiator. In an effort to provide some protection to the radiator, a specially strengthened armour cover was made available from the United States early in 1945. This weighed some 105lb and on balance it was decided that the small amount of protection afforded did not justify the additional weight and installation time.

The installation of elevator bobweights was an interim measure aimed at lessening the severity of dive recovery through increasing the stick pressure. Later P-51D and P-51K models had metal-covered elevators and a decreased angle of incidence in

the horizontal stabiliser to improve dive recovery at high speeds and lessen the risk of structural strain. It was planned to incorporate this change as a modification in all earlier P-51Ds and Ks. Structural damage continued to afflict the Mustang throughout its combat employment and, as has been mentioned previously, this was primarily due to the airframe being exposed to forces well in excess of those it was designed to meet. Bent Mustangs were not uncommon after engaging in combat; for example, the evidence with P-51D 44-13527 flown by Lt-Col Harold W. Scruggs, the deputy commander of the 339th Fighter Group, during air fighting on 29 June 1944. On return it was found that both wings of the aircraft exhibited pulled rivets and skin disruption in three places and the main spar was severely sprung. Scruggs's report ran:

'The initial attack on the enemy aircraft began with a split-S from 26,000ft down to approximately 15,000ft in which the airspeed was over 400mph. The pull-out was not abrupt. I felt considerable G but did not black out. The second combat ended with the enemy aircraft and myself in a vertical dive from 15,000ft to 3,000ft where pull-out was completed. I believe most of the damage to the airplane occurred during this last

manoeuvre. The airspeed was well over 400mph and the pull-out was sufficiently strong to tear the oxygen mask from my face. During the third and fourth combats, the airspeed was low and most manoeuvres were a series of "stall-turns" during which flaps were used. At one time I pulled the airplane in excessively and it did half an "outside snap roll" in which considerable negative G was exerted.' This period of fighting lasted 30min, during which Col Scruggs shot down two enemy fighters.

High speeds also produced trouble with gun bay and mainwheel covers. The gun bay covers on the upper surfaces of the wings became dislodged on early Merlin Mustangs during high-speed dives and pull-outs. The remedy was stronger securing latches. Again in January 1945 there were incidents of doors becom-

ing detached and a 450mph speed limit was imposed until this had been investigated. Mainwheel covers lifting at high speeds had been reported by RAF pilots at an early date and modifications were introduced to improve the securing latches. However, the redesign of the wing on the P-51D had incorporated changes in landing gear retraction, eliminating the safety up-locks. Two fatal accidents in England where a wing was shed revealed failure of the wheel doors leading to landing gear sag at high speeds, which in turn caused structural failure of the wing. This applied to the first 100 'D' models which were subsequently modified. Following production reinstated the up-locks, but these factory up-locks did not meet with complete satisfaction in Europe and an additional lock was added to ensure that the wheel-well doors were secured.

The ease with which a Merlin Mustang could enter a skid highlighted its lack of directional control — a characteristic which many pilots used to advantage in evading the enemy. The cut-down rear fuselage decking introduced on the P-51D required even more pilot vigilance with the rudder trim and led to the fitting of a dorsal extension to the tailfin to improve matters. The dorsal fin, to effect better direction stability, plus a change in trim tab linkage giving reverse boost to prevent over-control, were factory-fitted with the 201st and all subsequent 'D' models. Kits were eventually made available for similar dorsal fin installations on early 'D' and preceding models. No sooner had the dorsal fin appeared in combat units when an order of 13 July 1944 prohibited aircraft so equipped from engaging in slow rolls. Accidents in the United States had shown up a weakness in this fin, leading to buckling and the fin coming away in flight when subjected to the strain of slow rolling. Strengthening modifications were quickly effected and similar changes made on production.

As has been shown, changes in production to improve the breed often brought new problems in the field. Another instance was the pilot's seat which was altered in design to aid the installation of cockpit equipment and the quick detachment of the seat. This redesign incorporated several angles which, it was discovered, were given to catching on a pilot's parachute and dinghy straps when he attempted to bale out. Once again local modifications were put in hand to prevent this fouling.

While the revised gun installation on the P-51D and K models was a considerable improvement over that in the 'B' and 'C', there were still some instances of bullet trace jamming in the feed mechanism. The booster motors installed in the UK to overcome this problem were considered to be more trouble than they were worth. Eventually various improvements to the ammunition feed provided a fairly

high degree of reliability, but the effects of excessive 'G' on gun operation were never completely banished.

To improve the P-51's firepower in ground attack, serious consideration was given to the provision of gun packs that could be carried on the wing bomb racks and, if required, jettisoned in an emergency. Each pack carried two 0.50in guns with 340 rounds of ammunition per gun in a streamlined casing. The total weight was 450lb. However, the plan was never put into practice.

While many of the problems encountered in Europe were also faced in other theatres of war, the use of 100/130 fuel was standardised and the engine difficulties were minimal. Mustangs operated by other USAAFs

had carburettor air filters installed, a necessity where dusty and dirty airstrips were used. In tropical areas Mustang cockpits were found too hot and in need of improved ventilation. Repositioning of the fresh air ducts was carried out by many units to achieve better air circulation in the cockpit. A revised ventilating system was introduced on late production P-51Ds.

The Model N-3 reflector gunsight fitted in early Mustang production was found wanting by all users in the theatres of war in which it operated, chiefly through inaccuracy in all but the most favourable conditions. In Europe the British Mk II Starsight was substituted by most units; in other theatres the L-3 sight, originally developed for the P-38, was considered superior to the N-3. The same view predominated about the N-9 sight in the P-51D and this was often replaced by British models or by the L-3. Eventually the K-14 gyrosight won approval and replaced all other types when available.

In the China-India and Pacific war theatres which involved long-distance missions, Mustangs were modified at air depots to carry a direction-finding radio compass. A ring aerial, installed on top of the rear fuselage, could be traversed through 360° and thus enable the pilot to obtain directional bearings on commercial radio stations. Some of these aerials were enclosed within a plastic fairing of the type seen on bombers. The bearing was displayed on an instrument mounted in the cockpit.

Below:
Mass-production of a particular model did not necessarily give commonality of parts. Such was the variation of fit between supposedly identical engine inspection panels that in Europe it was policy to mark each with the number of the aircraft on which they fitted. This stemmed from mechanics removing and mixing panels from several aircraft and then having to try each panel until the speed screws lined up with the attaching holes in engine bearers.
Coffin With Wings, **P-51D 44-14322 of 364th Group, displays the last four digits of the serial, '4322' on five panels.** USAF

As an Eye in the Sky

Above:

The camera-carrying version of the P-51 was designated F-6 in the USAAF. Most early Merlin Mustang examples were conversions made at air depots. *Lady Patricia* of 161st Tac Recon Squadron, taxying out at Le Culot, Belgium, has a camera port for a K-24 in the fuselage side above the wing trailing edge. This aircraft had the fuselage fuel tank removed. USAAF

Above right:

Later conversions had two K-24 cameras, both placed in the fuselage just forward of the tailwheel compartment. One port was for a vertical and the other for an oblique-sighted camera, as on this F-6C of 111th Tac Recon Squadron at Dijon-Longuic in October 1944. Via S. Blandin

Right:

In Europe, commanders of several P-51 units had a K-22 camera installed on the fuselage support former behind the pilot seat. Shooting obliquely through the plexiglas canopy, they proved invaluable for photographing a unit's ground attack results and for impromptu photo reconnaissance over enemy territory. This is the installation in Lt-Col Bill Bailey's 352nd Fighter Squadron P-51D. USAAF

Above:

Factory installations on the F-6D, as with this 111th Tac Recon Squadron aircraft, had a port for a vertical camera forward of the tailwheel and another adjacent on the left side for obliques. Both these normally used K-24 cameras. Additionally a large port, higher in the fuselage side, usually sported a K-17. The K-17 took 9in×9in negatives and had 130 exposures and was effective up to 30,000ft. The K-24 took 5in×5in negatives and had 125 exposures and was excellent for high-speed low level photography or for heights up to 10,000ft. A. P. Clarke

Below right:

Good endurance and high performance made the Mustang highly suitable for tactical weather scouting. As these missions often involved only two aircraft in a hostile environment, these had to be fighter types to provide the best chances of surviving. The 9th Weather Reconnaissance Squadron (WRS) (Provisional) served the US 9th Air Force, its main function being to report weather conditions from target areas ahead of strike forces. Its original Mustangs were armed P-51Bs cast off by other units, but when the 9th AF's sole P-51 fighter group, the 354th, was forced to convert to P-47s due to a shortage of new Mustangs, the 9th WRS inherited many of the P-51Ds. This example still retains the blue and white 'starstud' nose marking of the 354th's 356th Squadron. The 'eight-oh' code was the 9th WRS official identification. A. R. Krieger

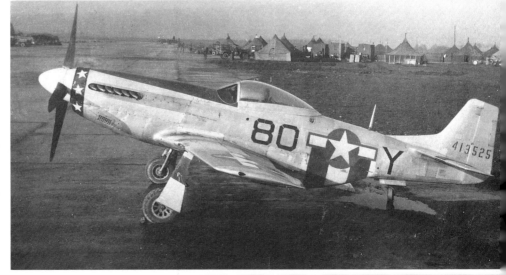

Appendix 1

USAAF P-51 Deployment in Theatres of War

● **ETO** — European Theatre of Operations was Western Europe, involving the 8th and 9th Air Forces and the 1st Allied Tactical Air Force.
● **MTO** — Mediterranean Theatre of Operations included North Africa, Italy, the Balkans and Mediterranean islands where the 12th and 15th Air Forces operated.
● **POA** — Pacific Ocean Area covered is in island groups across the central Pacific, notably the Hawaiian and Mariana groups with the 7th and 20th Air Forces.
● **FEAF** — Far East Air Forces comprised the 5th and 13th Air Forces in the New Guinea and Philippine Islands area.
● **CBI** — China-Burma-India theatre had the 14th Air Force in China and the 10th Air Force supporting operations from India and Burma
● Figures in brackets are *additional* Mustangs carried as F-6 photographic aircraft. All figures in the columns are for the end of each month but the method of assessment varied between war theatres. The ETO figures show only Merlin-engined fighter versions in the P-51 column. Allison P-51As are shown as F-6s (in brackets), although from January 1944 onwards conversions of Merlin Mustangs are included in the F-6 column and, later, production models. In the MTO figures the A-36A ground attack version is carried as P-51s and the P-51 with cameras as F-6s (bracketed). The first Merlin Mustangs are not included in the MTO P-51 column until March 1944 and by September 1944 the A-36 is eliminated. The sharp decline in F-6 numbers reflects the move of tactical reconnaissance squadrons to southern France. POA had no tactical reconnaissance or F-6 requirement. All figures relate to P-51D and K fighters. FEAF P-51 and F-6s were all Merlin-engined versions. CBI figures include Allison-engined P-51As. First P-51Bs are carried in February 1944.

	ETO		MTO		POA	FEAF		CBI	
Aug 43	—	*(18)*	231	*(51)*				70	
Sep 43	34	*(24)*	187	*(52)*				77	
Oct 43	159	*(23)*	163	*(49)*				82	
Nov 43	231	*(23)*	138	*(52)*				95	
Dec 43	266	*(36)*	133	*(48)*				100	
Jan 44	543	*(50)*	116	*(49)*				107	*(5)*
Feb 44	699	*(53)*	120	*(52)*				102	*(25)*
Mar 44	792	*(71)*	197	*(42)*				189	
Apr 44	950	*(87)*	225	*(57)*				193	
May 44	819	*(152)*	313	*(81)*				203	
Jun 44	803	*(138)*	481	*(84)*				204	*(8)*
Jul 44	1143	*(128)*	499	*(103)*				202	*(16)*
Aug 44	1177	*(153)*	411	*(86)*				209	*(17)*
Sep 44	1203	*(222)*	413	*(104)*			*(6)*	330	*(8)*
Oct 44	1366	*(304)*	430	*(13)*		41	*(15)*	295	*(15)*
Nov 44	1579	*(308)*	440	*(1)*	16	75	*(24)*	365	*(30)*
Dec 44	1548	*(292)*	491	*(4)*	203	95	*(22)*	383	*(33)*
Jan 45	1515	*(266)*	538	*(4)*	254	94	*(51)*	467	*(43)*
Feb 45	1576	*(251)*	510	*(4)*	247	261	*(47)*	421	*(83)*
Mar 45	1694	*(244)*	534	*(4)*	327	357	*(44)*	465	*(73)*
Apr 45	1867	*(254)*	588	*(5)*	388	373	*(46)*	458	*(73)*
May 45	1846	*(250)*	581	*(4)*	424	366	*(46)*	422	*(71)*
Jun 45	1728	*(247)*	551	—	379	465	*(48)*	472	*(68)*
Jul 45	1459	*(242)*	211	—	631	542	*(54)*	641	*(64)*
Aug 45	1361	*(210)*	7	—	767	502	*(76)*	621	*(56)*

Below:
An all-yellow empennage was the 52nd fighter Group dress. The P-51B has a sliding side-panel in the 'coffin hood'. S. Staples

Appendix 2

USAAF P-51 Disposition — June 1943 to August 1945

The following table shows the disposition of USAAF P-51s at the end of each month between June 1943 (when P-51B production got underway) and the end of hostilities. The first column shows the number of new Merlin-engined P-51s accepted from factories. However, the figures for the first three months are deceptive in that many airframes were without engines due to shortages. These figures include Mustangs to be delivered to the RAF and other Allied operators. The second, third and fourth columns include all model P-51s except the A-36 dive-bomber derived from the Allison-engined P-51A. The bracketed figures are *additional* Mustangs under the F-6 designation allotted to those fitted out with cameras for tactical reconnaissance operations. Until the summer of 1944, when batches of F-6Ds were incorporated in production, F-6s were conversions from P-51s and still carried under that designation. However, the precise number of camera-carrying Mustangs was never clear as conversions continued to be made in war zones without notification of change of designation.

V-1650 P-51 FACTORY ACCEPTANCE		P-51s ON HAND USAAF		P-51s ON HAND IN USA		P-51s OVERSEAS WITH USAAF	
Jun 43	20	298		260		29	
Jul 43	91	327		257		70	
Aug 43	175	438		344		94	
Sep 43	201	560		335		225	
Oct 43	284	720		382		338	
Nov 43	295	924		556		368	
Dec 43	332	1165		650		515	
Jan 44	370	1420		574		846	
Feb 44	380	1733		621		1112	
Mar 44	482	2027		535		1492	
Apr 44	407	2086		462		1624	
May 44	580	2484		675		1809	
Jun 44	581	2693		607		2086	
Jul 44	569	2733	(193)	615		2118	(193)
Aug 44	700	2799	(289)	613	(66)	2116	(223)
Sep 44	665	2933	(390)	695	(62)	2238	(328)
Oct 44	763	3341	(417)	726	(43)	2615	(374)
Nov 44	709	3666	(412)	748	(36)	2918	(376)
Dec 44	702	3914	(469)	842	(55)	3072	(414)
Jan 45	822	4338	(470)	1113	(53)	3225	(417)
Feb 45	704	4642	(448)	1150	(31)	3492	(417)
Mar 45	759	4802	(436)	998	(35)	3804	(401)
Apr 45	670	4833	(442)	923	(34)	3910	(408)
May 45	677	5192	(446)	1048	(53)	4144	(393)
Jun 45	701	5471	(466)	1409	(61)	4062	(405)
Jul 45	570	5541	(479)	1989	(87)	3552	(392)
Aug 45	208	5384	(470)	2283	(110)	3101	(354)

P-51Ds of 462nd Fighter Squadron over the western Pacific in July 1945, each nursing two 110gal drop tanks. Pilots are (from the camera) Lts Ed Linfante, Ed Bahlhorn and Jesse Sabin. Via E. Bahlhorn